GUS MACHADO'S AMERICAN DREAM

Memoirs

GUS MACHADO'S AMERICAN DREAM

®The Gus Machado FamilyFoundation

All Rights Reserved.

Translation: Benito García

Cover Design: Mario Carpio

Contents Graphic Design: Carpio Graphic Design

First Edition: August 2023. Miami, FL, USA.

ISBN 979-8328743105

All rights reserved. Total or partial reproduction, incorporation to a digital system or any other form in any media (electronic, mechanical, photocopy, recording or others) is not permitted unless previously authorized in writing by the Copyright holders.

To my daughters and sons Myra, Rudy, Lydia and Roberto, to all my grandchildren, and my great granddaughter and to my wife Lilliam, to my loyal associates and friends, and all the persons who influenced and helped me accomplish this marvelous American dream.

INDEX

Prologue	1
1. Cienfuegos, Cuba (1934)	4
2. Salemburg, North Carolina (1950)	17
3. Joliet, Illinois (1952)	29
4. Hialeah, Florida (1956)	41
5. Between Miami and Havana (1958-60)	53
6. New Horizons (1961-63)	63
7. Family, Business and Opportunities (1964-74)	74
8. An Explosive Decade (1970-79)	86
9. In the Major Leagues (1980-87)	104
10. A New Managerial Style (1988-1991)	124
11. Corporate Challenges (1992-2000)	144
12. My Life with Lilliam (2001)	160
13. Gus Machado's Legacy (2002-2021)	181
14. Finishing Touch: Gus Machado's Business School (2015-2021)	210
15. Epilogue: Memories of My Father	228

INTRODUCTION

This book is a combination of biography and autobiography of Gus Machado. It was written from numerous interviews with Gus, as well as family and friends over a period of more than four years, conducted by journalist Casto Ocando.

This is a collection of personal stories in Gus's life and of how life's challenging situations, as well as many unexpected opportunities, impacted changes in his professional and personal life.

Gus's life story demonstrates how the choices that we make in dealing with unexpected obstacles can influence our outcomes. It is also a testament to the power of a positive attitude and Gus's ability to find the opportunities in life's many unexpected events that are often beyond our control, and how to turn those events into wonderful opportunities.

Gus Machado sadly died on May 16, 2022 in his home at Grove Isle, Miami, surrounded by family and loved ones but his stories of his American Dream still live on.

PROLOGUE

A ll along my almost nine decades of life, by the grace of God, I underwent a varied range of situations and experiences that eventually shaped my character.

A good part of those experiences took place in the most prolific period of life, the 71 years that have gone since I arrived, for the time, as a student to a small locality in North Carolina.

Throughout that vast period of time, I lived basically in two locations: the first part was in Illinois, in the well-remembered city of Joliet, where I found my first job at the Caterpillar factories; and the second one in my beloved city of Hialeah, where I arrived in 1956 and founded the two main pillars of my existence: my family and my businesses.

These present memories are the product of my constant endeavors to sketch what my life has become along that time.

This sketch begins in the distant 1934, the year I was born in Caunao, a township on the outskirts of Cienfuegos. Then I go on to recount my trajectory in Cuba, and how a youthful prank changed my life and unexpectedly led the way to what has been my particular American Dream.

From the first time I set foot on American soil, in 1950, to the present, I have met a lot of people. Many have helped me to advance in this demanding journey. Others, I have helped. To all those who have been part of my life, even if they are not mentioned in this book, also goes my gratitude.

There are some people in particular whom I would like to mention because they were and still are in my life with everlasting links.

In first place, my children and grandchildren –to whom this book is dedicated–, who have been a fundamental reason in my life: Myra, my firstborn; Rudy, Lydia and Roberto.

Then, my dear wife, Lilliam, who not only has been my close life companion in the past two decades of my existence, but also an inspiration for countless endeavors described in this book.

To my partners, past and present, especially Víctor Benítez, a feisty manager with great foresight, who has been by my side in my enterprises for the past 34 years.

To my ever faithful and loyal friends, Fausto and Remedios Díaz.

To those who made possible the perpetuation of my legacy as a businessman and citizen, eager to be an example setter, especially to Monsignor Franklyn Casale and David A. Armstrong, former and current presidents of St. Thomas University, who honored me by naming the new and modern

Business School of that prestigious center of learning the Gus Machado College of Business.

To those I forgot to mention, once again my sincere gratitude.

I hope that this brief testimony of my life will be useful to those persons who struggled with all their might to accomplish, like I did, their most cherished American Dream.

1

Cienfuegos, Cuba (1934)

The moments of childhood and youthful years are never forgotten, just like your birthplace. Those moments and places are engraved in your memory. I was born in Cienfuegos province, in Cuba's southeast, on November 14, 1934, specifically in Caunao, a township on the outskirts of Cienfuegos, where we lived for generations. Cienfuegos always was a historical city, with extraordinary monuments, but above all the flavor of discovery, adventure and family.

There I was born and raised. There I learned my first lessons of life thanks to the dedication of my family and first teachers. There I discovered the world for the first time. And there I learned what my grandfather first and later my father had learned: to be an entrepreneur.

My family was not that large, but neither was it a small one. There were four of us: my father Eduardo Machado, my mother

Elia Hernández de Machado, my older brother Eduardo, Ed to us, and myself.

I remember that all our family lived in two houses near each other. The family was headed by a strong paternal figure, like an oak, my dear grandfather Rafael Calderín.

My grandfather Rafael was also born there. He was a hardworking man, highly energetic, who had a very productive farm, with a huge number of mango trees, and a long line of beehives that produced plenty of honey of the highest quality.

I grew up amidst the mango groves and surrounded by many bees, which I had to evade quite often in order to avoiding being stung by them.

My grandfather Rafael also had a commanding post in what was at the time called *Los Tanques*, the small power company that provided electricity for the area where we lived, in Caunao, and also lit up a large part of Cienfuegos, as well as supplying power to the sugar cane mills nearby.

He was responsible, along a crew of employees, for the upkeep of the power lines and energy flow, and it was not an easy task.

Perhaps without intending it, grandfather always conveyed to us that sense of responsibility and dedication to the assigned tasks.

Once he spoke to my brother, Ed Machado, and me, about the importance of being responsible. My grandfather used to take advantage of any occasion to convey to us a bit of his wisdom, a wisdom he did not acquire from studies but thanks to the hard and diligent work that marked his life.

"Once you are committed to a responsibility there's no going back. It has to be fulfilled in the best possible way," he would tell us often.

That was a lesson I learned early, and applied it to my own situation.

My grandfather Rafael was perhaps the mentor, the one who placed many things in my mind. He tried to help me in everything and was the family's businessman, an ability inherited by my mother, who had a lot of talent for business. And from there, of course, came my interest for business, something I have always had in my blood, as a family legacy.

My father, Eduardo, like my grandfather Rafael, was also a model of his own when it came to work and dedication. He became a master in sugar chemistry, and worked in a sugar cane mill near our home, a property of the Luzárraga family.

The Portugalete Sugar Mill was founded in 1873 and later acquired by the Luzárraga family in the early thirties.

The sugar cane mill was about 16 kilometers from Caunao, in the small town of Palmira, and was a great industrial complex with factories, centrifugal machines, hundreds of workers and with the capacity to process tens of thousands of *arrobas* (25 lbs.) of sugar cane per day.

It had its own railroad station, connecting it directly to the Port of Cienfuegos, and even its own telephone exchange. That's

GUS MACHADO'S AMERICAN DREAM, MEMOIRS | **7**

Young Gus, with his dear baseball cap and glove, with his parents Elia and Eduardo, and his older brother Ed, in Cuba.

where my papa worked.

In those days, Cienfuegos was a sugar hub in Cuba. It had an infrastructure that had been built over decades, including a railroad line that facilitated the transportation of sugar, and a great port for exports.

As expected, the communists wiped all that when Fidel Castro took over. But in my childhood days, it was a great center of business activity, developed around the sugar industry.

My papa was a man dedicated to his job. He used to leave early in the morning on his way to the sugar mill belonging to Mamerto Luzárraga, a 20-minute commute, and returned home shortly before dusk. That's how money was made to support the family.

He also worked in several other sugar mills, among them the Andreíta, which was in Cruces, and later at the Constancia, also belonging to the same owner, Luzárraga.

My papa was committed to teaching us to do things correctly. He gave me a number of house chores that I had to carry out. If I, by chance or carelessness, left any of those chores half way, my papa would make me finish what I had left undone, and as a punishment he would assign me some extra work.

"When you start doing something you have to finish it, and do it correctly," he used to tell me. It wasn't his intention to punish me, but he was very stern when it came to teaching us to be responsible, as demanded by our culture at the time.

My mother was very affectionate with us but also very strict.

A view of Gus' hometown Cienfuegos in the 1930s, in southern Cuba.

She was in charge of everything at home, day to day. She was zealous about our appearance, how we dressed, everything we did, and how we got along with everyone.

She never tired of telling us: "Don't do that because that's something that shouldn't be done," and that sort of things.

If you dared to ask: "Why this and why that?" my mother would reply with a stern look on her face: "Just because, because you have to do it and that's it, and don't bother to ask!" That's how mom was.

That was a time when kids could not loaf around all over doing nothing, and respect for the parents was something sacred.

My first steps in education

Due to many historical events, Cienfuegos has always had a special relationship with the United States, and above all with Florida.

Some of the battles between the U.S. Marines and the Spaniards took place in my city during the Spanish American War of 1898, and after the victory of the American forces, companies, professionals, missionaries and teachers started arriving to live in Cienfuegos. Of course, I learned that many years afterwards.

For some reason that has bearings with that past, my parents decided that I should study with the American missionaries that came from Florida to our city.

My first formal schooling took place in Cienfuegos, at the Eliza Bowman School, directed by the Ladies Division of the Methodist Church's General Board of Missions, based in New York.

At the age of five I began to study there from first to fourth grade. Classes were bilingual and taught by American teachers. There I took basic English, sciences and physical education, among other subjects.

Later I continued my studies in another famous school, Candler School, in Havana, an institution founded and ran by the American Methodist Church that was set on the island since the beginnings of the XX century, when Cuban troops, with key help from the American allies, expelled the Spaniards from the island.

The school was founded in 1919 by the initiative of Bishop Warren Candler, who arrived from Florida to establish several schools and churches in Havana and Cienfuegos, among other places, after 1898.

It was a highly prestigious school. Not everyone was admitted and it was a very demanding institution. It provided excellent education, although I can't say that it was better or worse than the Cuban public schools back then.

In that school they taught everything: not only basic math and language, as required by Cuban education authorities, but many other subjects and crafts such as choral music, typing, dressmaking and weaving. They also taught a subject that would eventually become very useful for me in the future: English.

Back then, there were many American companies operating in Cuba, and, of course, also in Cienfuegos, namely a slew of sugar cane mills spread all over the province, such as the Portugalete sugar mill, where my father worked, and others, such as the Manuelita, and the Dos Hermanos (Two Brothers).

Since many American families who lived there sent their kids to the Candler School, besides living along with them and thus learning the language I also had the opportunity to pick up a lot about the American culture.

We had a good house in the neighborhood of El Vedado, in Havana, where I lived while going to fifth, sixth and seventh

Young Gus during his teens in Cuba.

grades. To this day I still have a lot of memories about those years.

It was really easy for me to learn English because I started at an early age. In the beginning it was the quick lessons in which you were taught: "*chica* is girl and *muchacho* is boy." Followed by conversations and that helped me become more familiar with the language.

A marvelous childhood

Notwithstanding the rigidity and discipline of life with my parents and grandparents, I had a fortunate and happy childhood. I have many good memories from that stage in my life.

Fortunately, my father had a good position thanks to his technical job as a master chemist in the sugar industry and mom took care of the house. All went well because they were a divine couple.

At home, for example, traditions were well observed, above all those involving gifts, as in birthdays or Three Kings Day, which is when the Christmas gifts arrived.

Although I attended a Methodist school, our family was considered catholic, like the majority of Cuban families of that time.

One of our most enjoyed activities was going to a baseball game. My father was a baseball fan, and the Cienfuegos team, of the Cuban National League, had plenty of devotees. And my father used to take us all, mom included, to the ballpark.

I enjoyed those games enormously. It was a fanship I never gave up, and I shared it with my papa. My brother, instead, was never much of a sports fan. He didn't feel the same way; he was more into philosophy and intellectual reading. But I really loved baseball and so did my papa.

At some point in my childhood, I dreamed of becoming a baseball player. That sport's fanship in Cienfuegos was quite strong, and it wasn't for nothing. As I would learn later in life, Cuba was practically the second country in the world, after the United States, to establish a baseball league and play it with great enthusiasm. And the Cienfuegos team became one of the firsts.

Besides baseball there was something else that I enjoyed a lot: buying and selling.

I loved going out with mom to help her while shopping. And I was thrilled to see what merchants were doing: buying something here and selling it there, for profit.

I began to try my luck in business while in high school. It all started at my grandfather Rafael's farm. It was huge. In there, my grandfather had the beehives that produced honey, and a large mango plantation.

When I visited him, my grandfather would tell me: "Come and learn." And showed me how honey was collected. Many a sting, by the way, did I suffer during those trips, but I must admit that I learned a lot about the business of running a thriving farm.

And there, right away, I caught the drift, because my grandfather also sold his products in the market to make some extra money, and accompanying grandpa, who always took me along, taught me what it took to be businessman.

Later on, besides the honey and the fruits, my grandfather began to sell meat from the cattle he also had at the farm. But for that we didn't have to go to the market, the buyers came to the farm for the meat. The meat was tops, judging from what I heard from the people who came to buy it.

Another successful business started in my family was my mother's idea. With my papa's backing, they bought another house right in Cienfuegos and turned it into a boarding house, for renting to girls from the surrounding townships that came to school in the city.

The rent was paid by those girl's parents. And for that it was my older brother who helped mom, with great discretion. Mom always kept the distance between us and the girls. But that business generated a tremendous income for the family.

Those were wonderful years. While still in school, on the weekends I would sell fruits from my grandfather's farm. I was very active and also had a social life. I had girlfriends and liked dancing. Although mom kept me somewhat on a leash, I cannot forget those years because I was very happy then.

A bunch of kids that changed my life

During my school years I had a circle of friends that met regularly to do things together.

We liked to go out and explore, share stories, go to baseball games and tell jokes. It was a wholesome time and there was no malice, although every now and then we were quite capable of misbehaving and incurring in a silly thing or two. One time I had the idea of organizing an outing with my friends. I thought it would be a good opportunity not only to enjoy the ride but to make some money on the side by charging for the fare.

The idea seemed good to me, so I shared it with my friends, who reacted with their total approval.

We were all excited about the prospect of the trip, which was to be made on the bus that took us to and from school. We were planning to charge a peso per passenger.

This ride, an idea of happy-go-lucky kids, turned out however into the beginning of another adventure that none of us were able to imagine at the moment.

It was the first event that, unexpectedly, changed my life forever.

2

Salemburg, North Carolina (1950)

The first episode of my existence that changed my life completely took place when I was finishing my studies at the Candler School, of the Methodist missionaries, in Cienfuegos.

At the school where I was studying, I had a group of friends, kids like myself, although we were slightly older.

It was a diverse group, very enthusiastic and, let's say, without malice. We used to hang around, to explore, and to chat among ourselves. In a few words, it was a group of young men who liked to have a good time.

At the time there was a bus, what we called *guagua* (in the Cuban vernacular) that carried students attending the school. The *guagua* passed by picking us up early in the morning and dropped us off in the afternoon in front of our respective homes.

After a while I befriended the driver, named Luis, and joined him along all the routes that the *guagua* traversed throughout the city.

One day, I convinced Luis to take me and a small group of students for a ride to the beach.

I told him that it was part of a school activity, and that we had permission from the school, but the truth was that we were the only ones who knew about that ride.

It occurred to me that I could make a profit on the side, and started charging a *peso* per student. All my friends approved it, and we agreed to get together after school.

On the day of the trip my friends and I met outside the school, as agreed. Luis, the driver, had already finished all the day's routes and was punctually waiting to pick us up.

I remember planting myself at the entrance to the *guagua*, and began to collect the *peso* from each student.

When all of us were on board, Luis began to start the engine of the *guagua*, and we were already imagining ourselves enjoying the surf.

At last, the engine started and began to move very slowly. Just at that point we heard someone shouting imperatively:

"Stop that bus right now!" ordered the hectic voice.

All the kids turned around immediately to see what was happening. The driver, with fear on his face, stopped dead the guagua, slammed on the hand brake and went out of the *guagua*.

When the person who had been screaming and chasing us

approached the bus, we realized that it was none other than the school principal.

"We got caught," I muttered.

The principal went inside the *guagua* and when he asked who was responsible, everyone pointed to me.

"Good-bye to the beach and all the *pesos*," I thought.

The incident did not result in my expulsion, but something worse.

Besides the sharp scolding, not only from the principal but from my mother as well, that I would never forget, I was informed of the punishment:

It was then and there that my parents let me know that they had decided to send me to a school where I would not be allowed to step outside. I asked myself how that could be possible, considering that what I had done was not so serious after all.

But there was no way out. My new destination was a military academy in the United States.

From the very beginning, the thought of leaving Cuba did not sit well with me. But there was no alternative. Saying "no" to my mother, or stating my disagreement, was unthinkable. And like a good kid who understands the consequences of his actions, I accepted my fate.

Later I learned that everything had been planned by my dear mother. With great effort she was trying to give the best education possible to my brother Ed and myself.

A photo of the Edward Military Institute taken in 1950,
a year before Gus' admittance.

My mother got Ed a scholarship to study in a Methodist School in the United States, because he was thinking about studying to become a religious minister.

Since I did not have that kind of vocation, my mother sent me to the military academy I mentioned.

Shortly after I shipped out with a small suitcase, on my way to the Marianao airport, to leave Cuba for the first time. There I boarded an Aerolíneas Q plane, with a $20 ticket for the short round trip Havana- Key West.

Upon arriving I found a Greyhound bus waiting to depart for a marathonic 16-hour trip to my new destination: Salemburg, North Carolina.

Life had changed completely for me.

My new life at the Edwards Academy

Later on, I found out that after the *guagua* incident with Luis the driver and the school principal, my mother was alarmed and immediately sought a way to, so to speak, inject me with more discipline.

I have no doubts that she was looking for the best way for me to grow up as an upstanding man, and she believed that she had found the best solution.

Apparently the very same Methodist missionaries in Cienfuegos recommended enrolling me at the North Carolina military academy, built in 1926 by a Methodist minister,

Gus and Lilliam Machado during their 2021 visit to the historical Pineland College, Edward Military Institute, where Gus studied in the '50s.

Anderson Edwards, who invested all his lifetime savings into building the institution, that being was named after him.

At the age of 16, that destination seemed to me another adventure. I, being an optimist and open to novelties since my age of reason, undertook the experience as a challenge.

During the trip from Key West to North Carolina, I noticed something that I had never seen and it caught my attention.

When I boarded the Greyhound bus, there were two or three white passengers seating up front and about five or six blacks sitting at the rear of the bus. It caught my attention because I was not aware of what was going on.

Then I decided to sit in the middle of the bus, being half empty, and there I remained quietly until I reached the last stop.

When we made a stop and I went out to go to the restroom and later get a soda, I saw signs reading *"Black"* or *"Colored,"* and *"White."* It piqued my curiosity because in Cuba we did not have that type of discrimination between blacks and whites.

Upon arriving, after the long trip, I was impressed by the imposing building shaped like a medieval castle, housing the headquarters of the Edwards Military Institute, a school dedicated to training the military as well a "straightening out" mischievous brats like myself.

Needless to say, back then there were no Hispanics in that part of the United States. Not even Mexicans. The only one in the entire academy was another Cuban named Luis Díaz, who had been there for a year.

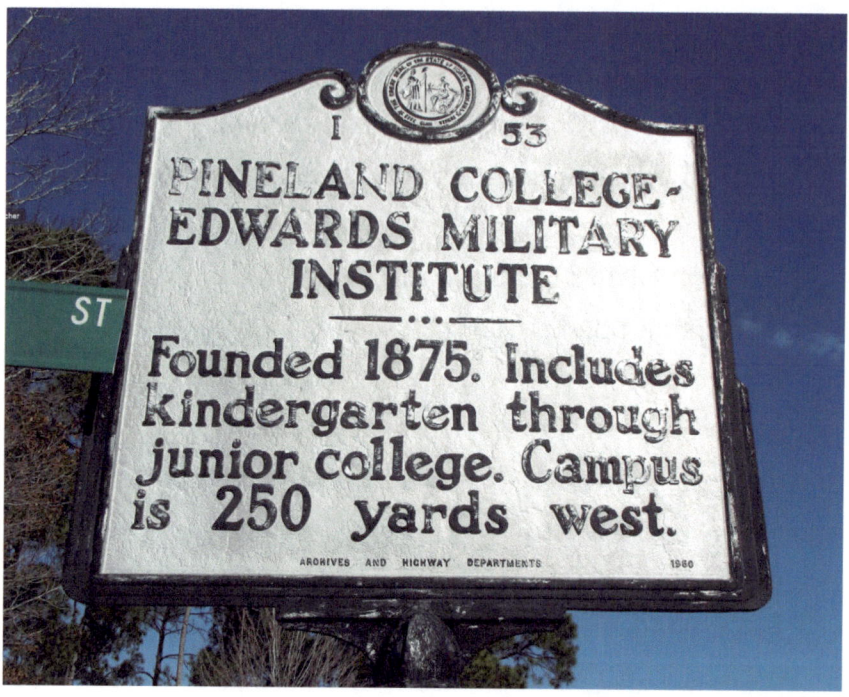

The Pineland-Edwards Institute was a prominent educational center established in 1875 in North Carolina, where an elite of students were formed as leaders of the future.

Fortunately, when I met Luis, he spoke to me in Spanish, and explained to me the institute's rules, which he already knew. He told me: "This is like this, and this is like that." He helped me a lot, although we were living in different buildings, and I was surrounded by Americans.

The institute was actually a building complex, with class rooms, conference rooms, a large library, and dorms for the resident students.

It also had wide outdoor areas for sports, such as football

and baseball; a large indoor area where students practiced all sorts of military formations and marches.

As expected, the lifestyle was kept at firm pace: up at dawn, exercise, personal hygiene, long class hours, marches and countermarches, and sparse leisure time. Everything ran at such a quick pace that you didn't even have time to miss your family.

Although I already had some knowledge of English from my bilingual classes at Candler, it was at the Edwards academy where I gained command of the language.

The life experience at the academy came as a shock. Coming from a Cuban provincial city with a relaxed daily routine, I had to adapt to a totally different pace of life, and that meant an effort that I was not used to.

Another change was the interaction with new classmates who came with their own family and cultural traditions, very different from mine. And the worst part: no girlfriends, dances or adventurous rides.

However, I think that that experience was very advantageous for me. I believe that my parents made the right decision. It taught me discipline and concentration. It taught me to be a better person, and appreciate the consequences of our actions. Because, there with me, were other kids of my age, all of them Americans, who had had their own problems, or had run away, and were doing their possible best to mend their ways.

One of the things I liked was the parades and marches. We

were given fake rifles, called *dummies*, and we had to march holding the rifle on the right or left shoulder, depending on the routine, and we had to chant like they do in the army. We were all rather young and enjoyed all that very much.

The Edwards academy experience showed me a lot of things I ignored. From a distance, it made me appreciate my family's value. It forced me to integrate my Cuban legacy with the American way of life. The result of that mixture marked my life deeply, and its benefits began to show years later, when I launched myself to make my entrepreneur's dreams a reality.

That experience also taught me that the best thing that can happen to a teenager who doesn't want to get along in school is military schooling.

Because they teach you regulations and discipline, and that gave me bearings in life, something for which I have to be grateful to my parents.

My return to Cuba and a fortuitous meeting

The winter of 1950 was very slow for me. I missed like never before the warm breeze blowing from the Cienfuegos Bay in summer. The joy of snow gave way to dark and cold days, typical of the winter season. But my spirit, far from getting depressed, was reverberating with the Caribbean effervescence that has always characterized me.

Then came spring and the military pace that had seemed

so brunt at first, turned bearable. The secret was quite simple: as the Cuban saying goes: *No cojas lucha que la caña es mucha* (Dont' get flustered, there's plenty of sugar cane to cut).

When the summer of 1951 came, I registered at another school, called Greenville College, near Salemburg. I was finishing high school, and by then I had learned English and was getting along just fine.

Finally, on December 1951 I was able to travel for the holidays. Again, the long 16-hour trip by bus to Key West, from there the Aerolíneas Q plane to Havana, where my parents were waiting to take me home to Cienfuegos.

When I arrived at my city after a long time away, I don't know if things had changed, or it was I who changed during those months spent in the United States.

Be as it may, I enjoyed it as much as I could, because I would be returning to school in the first weeks of January 1952.

I shared my time with old friends from school, I visited my grandfather's farm, with his abundant supplies of merchandise to sell at the market, and once or twice I went out to shake a leg because dancing has always been my weakness.

Eventually, it was time for farewells and my mother allowed her sadness to emerge on my going away again. By now the prank involving the *guagua*, the driver, Luis, and the school principal seemed something from a distant past. Nevertheless, I had to finish my education as planned.

This time a friend of the family drove me to Havana to

take a plane to Key West. The trip was normal. I would have preferred to stay in Cienfuegos, but a part of me made me think of my future possibilities if I continued my education in North Carolina.

While the plane crossed the Florida Strait on the way to Key West, I thought about the possibilities I had ahead of me.

I felt that I was capable of making my own decisions. I was coming of age, which in Cuba was 18 years, although I did not have any concrete plans.

Once in Key West I walked to the bus station to take the *guagua* that would bring me back again to Salemburg, North Carolina.

I walked up the steps and showed the ticket to the driver of the *guagua*. It was there, while walking to find my seat that the second episode that changed my life completely happened.

Just like the first episode that had serious consequences for my life, everything took place in a *guagua*, and neither time did I expect what was about to happen.

3

Joliet, Illinois (1952)

I had just boarded the Greyhound bus that day of January 1952 in the Key West bus station. Her face grabbed my attention. The girl was sitting at the back of the *guagua*, looking out casually through the window. The seat next to her was empty.

I remembered having seen her before on the plane, but I had not paid much attention to her.

"She's a very pretty girl," I thought. Without wasting any time, I sat next to her. She didn't flinch at first.

"Good afternoon," I introduced myself extending my hand, and flashing my best smile: "Gus Machado, at your service."

She didn't decline my hand, and with a serious countenance, replied: "Good afternoon. Olga Garrote, nice to meet you."

Immediately I noticed that her Spanish sounded different. I seized the opportunity to continue the conversation.

"What part of Cuba are you from?" I ventured.

"I come from Havana. My parents live there," said Olga, and showing interest in continuing the chat, added:

"Before we lived in Spain," she explained. "My family came to Cuba to get away from the war," she added somberly, referring to the ravages of World War II and the Spanish Civil War.

In no time we were so involved in a lively conversation that we didn't notice that the bus had departed towards Miami. While I was going to North Carolina, her destination was Oklahoma, where she enrolled in a secretarial program.

The dialog was pleasant and she felt confident enough to talk about her family history.

She told me that her father, José "Pepe" Garrote, was an outstanding plastic artist in Havana, who participated in the artistic decorations of the Capitol when it was remodeled during General Gerardo Machado and Morales' regime, and added that as a sculptor he had a knack for gargoyles.

She went on to tell me that her grandfather had worked in the Havana Museum of Art and Natural History, and added that she herself, besides painting, was into dancing and singing.

"I like art. And also write poetry," she added.

I couldn't get over my amazement by the luck I had on that trip.

Like me, she was coming from Cuba and going to a boarding school to study. Not for a matter of discipline but because her parents wanted her to have a good education.

Olga Garrote de Machado, Gus' first wife, in the splendor of her youth in Cuba.

For me the trip ahead was a long one, but not for her, whose final destination was the Miami bus station, and time was flying.

So, I decided to act fast.

Thus began my first engagement

I dared to place a hand on her left leg over the flowered print dress she was wearing, to test the waters, so to speak.

But Olga made a quick gesture of surprise.

"But... just what do you want?" she said, firmly moving my hand away from her lap.

Without taking my eyes away from her, I leaned over trying to hug her, and blurted:

"I want to kiss you."

She was amazed by the speed in which the events were going, and asked again:

"What do you want?"

"To kiss you," I replied as I moved my face closer to hers.

"If you want anything with me, first we have to get married," she said flatly, looking at me straight in the eye.

"I'll get married, I'll marry you," I replied without a thought. "Let's get married."

We already had several hours of travel, so we got down from the bus on the next stop, Miami.

We spent the night in a hotel and the next morning we went to the court house to get married. When we were before the

Gus Machado was always an attentive father with his kids.

judge, she showed her identification –she was a few years older than I – and I showed my passport. The judge looked at it and said we could not get married because I was not 18 years old, and according to Florida law I would need parental permission.

Olga did not have that problem; she was of age and therefore not restricted by anything other than her own will.

Then, someone suggested we continue our trip to the next state, Georgia, where my age would be no impediment for marriage.

I was a few months shy of eighteen, and once again on the verge of a new milestone that would change my course in life.

Young to marry, on to a working life

Was I really in love with that woman? Was I aware of the transcendental decision made in the heat of a conversation during a trip on a *guagua* next to a beautiful woman?

I certainly did not have the time to answer those questions, because Olga's excitement with the anticipation of a new life was as strong as mine. Perhaps it was the perspective of our loneliness in a country that we had barely begun to assimilate to and understand. Or perhaps it was simply the magic of love at first sight.

Whatever it was, we began the second part of the trip towards Georgia. At present, many years afterwards, some details of the brief ceremony escape my memory. But I recall rather well that

Gus and his first wife Olga, recently married, in 1952.

Gus holds his first-born daughter Myra while his mother Elena, visiting from Cuba, holds Rudy in her arm at the house that Gus was building in Jolliet, Illinois, in 1954.

after we tied the knot, she called her parents and I called mine, to let them know what we had done.

From a telephone booth in a remote Georgia town, I placed a long distance call to my papa Eduardo. For me it was a man to man. Without any preambles, I told him:

"I got married."

My papa, after a brief silence on the line, said:

"I hope you know what you're doing," and then added: "If you have a wife, then get a job."

I replied with all due respect that I was ready to do whatever was necessary to support my wife and any forthcoming children. Fortunately, he took the idea of my marriage more naturally than I had expected.

Olga was very happy. After getting married, she continued her trip to Oklahoma, to finish her secretarial studies, and I continued studying for the next six months until I graduated at Greenville College.

Then I called my brother Ed, who was studying in Illinois, where he also had a job. He told me:

"Well, here you can find a job. They are opening positions in a large factory that is about to open."

My first children, in Joliet, Illinois

After talking to Ed, I began to organize everything to settle in Joliet, the city where he was living.

Gus and Olga Machado during a picnic in Jolliet, Illinois, with his first daughter Myra and the family dog.

In the six months after my wedding with Olga I put my things in order to move to Joliet and find a job at the Caterpillar Tractor Company which was interviewing prospective employees.

Olga stayed in Oklahoma waiting for me to find a place for us to live.

The morning after I arrived in Joliet, in late summer of 1952, I went for an interview at Caterpillar, and they took my application.

I was lucky because right then and there I was hired for a janitorial job, sweeping and cleaning the factory, with a salary of between 75 cents and 1.25 dollars per hour.

It wasn't a bad salary, if you consider that in those days one could buy a house in the Joliet suburbs for less than $5,000. A brand new Ford Crestliner car, for example, cost around $1,600. Gas was 27 cents per gallon. Life was even cheaper than in Cuba.

So, I began sweeping with great discipline, because I no longer had my parents' financial support, and didn't have the training to operate any machines. Early every morning I grabbed my broom, and made sure that everything was clean and in place.

At the time, Caterpillar was a young corporation (founded as such in 1925), and growing. Every day new workers were added at the assembly lines for tractors and the new machinery for moving soil and building highways, and those were selling like hot cakes everywhere around the globe.

The first months I lived with my brother Ed, not having to pay rent and thus saving money to bring Olga from Oklahoma.

After two or three months I had saved enough money to rent a small apartment and called Olga telling her to pack her things and come with me.

I must say that my brother Ed helped me a lot, not just in helping me get a job but giving me a hand in starting my own family.

A short time after I started, my supervisor at Caterpillar informed me that I would be receiving a special training and then, after six months on the job, I began to operate a parts-making machine, not only manufacturing them but also making sure that there no flaws or imperfections.

In a matter of few months, I was making $1.50 per hour, so I started thinking seriously about buying my first home. Shortly thereafter I bought a lot and built a house, just in time for the arrival of the newcoming children.

The first one was Myra, born on February 21, 1953, less than a year than we had been living in Joliet. Her birth was a blessing, giving me a tremendous motivation to continue improving on my job, with the illusion of making a reality of that much talked about American Dream in those days.

The next year, my second child, Rudy, was born on April 19, 1954, the first son, bringing further joy at home. A year after that, on May 21, 1955, the third one, my daughter Lydia, came to this world.

Although our financial situation was booming, we were still nostalgic about missing Cuba. We always remembered the good old times and Cienfuegos's great climate, when compared to the harsh winters of that part of Illinois, near Lake Michigan.

In less time that I had foreseen, I had a larger family than the one I was born in, integrated just by my brother Ed and I.

Barely a few years after the *guagua* incident in Cuba, I realized how much my life had changed. Over that brief period of time I had learned the discipline of military life, and a new life style in another country; I married, had formed a home, found my first job and now was the proud father of three kids born in this new world in which I had the luck to live.

But the changes did not stop there. New circumstances opened another chapter in my life in this country of opportunities, with new difficulties but also new challenges that I was eager to face.

4

Hialeah, Florida (1956)

Four years after my arrival in Joliet, and with a flourishing family, came the start of a new stage.

During that time of continuous work and taking on the responsibilities of forming and making my own family, I found myself meditating more often about my future, and what I really wanted to do with my life.

I felt that with 22 years and three kids, time was ripe to search for new goals and make my aspirations a reality.

Several factors had a crucial influence: one of them was the bitter cold that made life more difficult in Joliet, something to which I could never adapt myself completely.

Also, for my wife Olga it was very difficult to endure the bitter cold, and she never stopped reminding me of that.

Another factor was my conviction that I was ready to try my luck with new opportunities, even my own business, although I was doing very well at Caterpillar.

That was when, early in 1956, we made the decision to move to Florida. Of course, the proximity of Miami to Havana was another factor attracting Olga, who had not seen her parents in years. So, after putting the house up for sale, I resigned from my job at Caterpillar and we undertook a long journey by land to South Florida.

We finally arrived at Miami in the spring of that year. Previously we had arranged a rental in the area of Opa-Locka, north of Hialeah, where we would be staying until we reorganized this new stage of our lives.

More than six years had run by since leaving Cuba and in that time I had evolved from being a mischievous student to becoming a family man, father of three, and one more on the way. As a matter of fact, by the time we reached Hialeah, my wife Olga was pregnant with the one that would be our fourth and last child, Robert, the only one of our kids born in Florida.

Hialeah was then a small town surrounded by large cattle ranches. The owners of these lands were the Graham family, which had among them several prominent members, such as State Senator Ernest Graham, the *Washington Post's* Editor, Phillip Graham; and Florida Governor and later Federal Senator Bob Graham.

Shorty after Robert's birth, on July 30, 1956, Olga and I agreed that it was time to find help with the family.

It was no easy task for her to deal with four kids and mind

Lydia, Robert, Rudy and Myra at home in Hialeah in the late 1950s.

the house work, while I was trying to bring home the necessary income.

One fine day in August, Olga boarded a *guagua* to Key West with all the children coming along, and from there to Havana, where her parents were awaiting with open arms.

For Myra, just three; Rudy, two and one-year-old Lydia, it was a great experience. They still remember that trip: it was the first they met their maternal grandparents.

After Olga's temporary departure, I immediately began to look for a job, while getting along to know the city. I wanted to gain time to find business opportunities in the area.

Meanwhile, I got a job driving a dump truck, which I knew how to drive because I had worked constructing them at Caterpillar. I worked at that driving job for six months and by then I already had rented a house.

Such were my first months in South Florida, and that was the job that allowed me to support my growing family.

In my mind, however, I had a goal: to do whatever was possible to set up my own business, and to do what thrilled me since I was a kid: buy and sell products.

The opportunity arrived randomly, but it set a path that I would never be able to leave.

My first business with a $2,000 loan

Hialeah, "The City that Progresses," was not even the shadow of what it is today, but just a little town north of Miami. It was a young township, founded in 1925, just 30 years before, but it promised a very dynamic future.

It was a time in which you could count the Hispanics with the fingers in one hand, and to hear anyone on the streets speaking Spanish with a Cuban accent was truly rare.

Hialeah was growing in an organized manner, with subdivisions of land for private ownership everywhere, efficiently built, with wide streets and budding industrial and commercial zones, like Flamingo Plaza, and attractions like the

La Carreta restaurant in Hialeah was one of Gus Machado's favorite places. He had a table always reserved for him there.
Gus considered Hialeah, the city where he grew up as a top-notch businessman, as Gus Machado's territory.

Hialeah Race Track, the famous racecourse that was a meeting point for tourists as well as residents from elsewhere in Dade County and the State of Florida.

You could notice the prosperity by driving around the Hialeah streets. Business activities as well as human and car transit were everywhere, a good sign that money was flowing, something that encouraged me to jump in the water on my own.

Then I began to search for business opportunities, and found a Sinclair gas station, on Miami Avenue and 17th Street, in North Miami. It was closed but had a sign in English reading: "For information call such and such number."

I called and was told that they were interested in renting the gas station. "You are renting it?" I asked again.

"Yes," came the answer.

I had a small capital from the profits of selling the house in Joliet.

Determined to make my dream of becoming an entrepreneur in the United States a reality, I asked for help from my papa in Cuba, with whom I had a good relationship despite everything.

My papa Eduardo not only showed his disposition to support me, but also trusted my potential for business.

With my meager savings plus the $2,000 my papa lent me, I rented the Sinclair station and began working as my own boss.

Immediately I noticed that the gas station had a good flow of customers, to fill the tank as well as to order oil changes and brake repairs or any other mechanical problems, because it also had a repair shop.

I dedicated myself body and soul to this business. At last, I

A view of Hialeah in 1957, when Gus Machado was beginning to succeed as entrepreneur.

had something of my own, something I could struggle for and make it thrive. An instrument to show my capacity, to learn the complex tasks of being an entrepreneur, and a path for growth for me and my family. I believe that there I had found my vocation for business.

It was the beginning of my American Dream.

I get into the used car business by chance

Around that time my parents were visiting us from Havana and spending a spell with us. I rented for them an apartment about four or five blocks from the station, and my papa, who came to see me when he was not working in the sugar *zafra* in Cienfuegos, helped me at the station.

At first, work was a seven-days-a-week affair. The gas station basically had several fuel pumps, a repair shop, and a small store where customers went to pay. That little store had a counter and a few shelves in the back, those were empty most of the time and that made a bad impression.

At the time I had spent all the money I had on a new underground gas tank for the station, and had nothing left to buy replacement parts to sell.

It was then that I had an idea. As it turned out a few blocks away was an auto parts store where we bought the replacements needed to make repairs. And behind that store there was always a bunch of empty boxes from the auto parts, new boxes thrown in the trash. There were all kinds of boxes, because they had a large inventory.

Then, one day I started picking up those empty new boxes, and placing them on the shelves at the back of my store, with rocks inside. Those boxes looked pretty, so much so that the customers got the impression that the store was well stocked.

Every day customers came in looking for help with all kinds of repairs, and there was always work.

For those jobs I had help from a Cuban mechanic I had met elsewhere, and brought him to work with me. My papa also helped around when he was visiting us.

At the time I didn't know, but the station was located in an area where many Puerto Ricans came to work during the winter tourist season, before going to New York for the summer.

That meant a floating population that came and went, and from it came the clientele that enhanced my business, because they would fill up, and bring their vehicles for maintenance and repairs, and that was the way I really got into in the repair business.

One time, a customer brought in a vehicle that needed a major engine overhaul. It just so happened that the car was raised about five feet above the floor on a hydraulic platform, so the mechanics could examine it and work below the engine, when the car tilted and fell to one side.

Thank God several people who were passing by came to help and we were able to straighten up the car, but the roof was squashed.

The vehicle belonged to a Puerto Rican customer, and thinking that he was not going to like what had happened, I came up with a possible solution.

I offered the customer to exchange the car for a similar one, which meant I would have to look for a used car with the same features. Another customer had recently offered to sell me his Chevrolet convertible, so I explained the situation to the Puerto Rican and offered a deal to solve the problem.

At first the Puerto Rican did not want to make a deal and wanted to call the insurance company. But back then I had no insurance, it wasn't like now, the laws were different. Finally, he accepted and we went ahead with the transaction.

That was the first car I sold in my life.

And so, literally by accident, I got started in the business of buying and selling used cars, and luckily, many other options in that trade that I had never imagined opened up.

My first experiences as an automotive entrepreneur

When I sold that first vehicle, I invested a little bit of money in another pair of used cars, and that's how I got started in the car business.

Before putting them for sale, I had the mechanics check them completely to make sure that I would not be selling a deficient product. I was always concerned with taking care of my reputation. In the long run, that's what you need to succeed.

The business turned out to be a blessing. It took off right away. The cars were sold for between $100 and $300, and there were some customers that got small bank loans to buy them.

I started selling a car per week, and I had the discipline of investing each cent from those sales in more used cars. In a short time, I had up to 10 used cars to show, the most I could have for sale in the limited parking space of my business place.

That was when I had the idea of dedicating myself exclusively to buying and selling used vehicles. That was where the real deals were.

Selling gas meant a little profit per gallon. Repairs were doing well since I had a good customer flow every week, but it was a more complicated service because I had to deal with the mechanics and sometimes with customers that were not all that satisfied.

Instead, the pure and simple sale of vehicles was something that could grow without complications other than the paper work. Cars were sold as is, and since the cars were in good working order, a satisfied customer brought in another one, and that's how business grew because a good reputation helps.

I remember those days quite well. Everybody wanted to have a car. Those were the post-war years, and we had a good recovery promoted by President Dwight Eisenhower.

The fast-selling models were Chevrolets, particularly the Chevy Bel Air, a car with a high demand; and the Styleline, a

Aerial view of the city of Hialeah in the late '50s, when Gus Machado's businesses in Miami began to grow.

well-built and solid machine.

For me selling used cars was an exciting job. Early each morning, after tidying up my small desk behind the store counter (with the empty boxes on the shelves) I went out to supervise the repairs in the shop, and then, dusting and polishing a bit the cars on sale, before the customers began showing up.

The job of dealing with people was like a gift for me. As important as the quality of the product sold is the attention that the seller should pay to the buyer. A smile, a hand shake, a nice comment can do marvels and multiply the sales.

Much of what I learned in those first days of my venturing

into business, I put to practice successfully in the many deals I made later, in over 60 years of my career as entrepreneur.

It is said that enjoying work is not a job but a passion. I know perfectly well what that expression means, because I've lived it along my life.

My first expansion attempt

Some people were surprised by my accent, or upon learning that I was born in Cuba, and were curious about it. As incredible as it might sound, back then it wasn't as common as it became later to find Cubans in Miami.

However, while getting around I was meeting more people and some fellow countrymen living in Miami.

I was also getting acquainted with the Puerto Rican community that came during the tourist high season, to work in the Miami Beach hotels –long before settling down in New York–, and eventually became a part of my regular clientele.

Used car sales were moving in an impressive way. The business was just growing. The next step for me was becoming quite clear: expanding to new markets.

But that meant risks. And I was quite ready to take that challenge.

5

Between Miami and Havana (1958-60)

Life in Hialeah was certainly more comfortable than in Joliet, especially because there was no ice in winter.

I lived with Olga and the kids in East Hialeah. The Palmetto Expressway was nothing even close to a highway but more like a bare bones two- way road.

The kids were adapting well to their studies, while I was striving to increase sales and get to know other people in the trade, aiming to find possible associates or new markets.

There weren't many Hispanics in Miami, but perhaps just a growing Puerto Rican and Cuban community. Once in a blue moon you found someone from South America, like the time I had an Ecuadorian customer who bought many vehicles for reselling.

Back then there were just a few business owned by Latinos, who spoke Spanish but were nevertheless adapted to the

American system.

I myself was eager to adapt to the surrounding society and culture. I was zealously trying to integrate into the American society. I understood that unless I accepted and practiced the American way of life, including the best possible command of the language, I would never attain the success I was striving for.

I remember the days of arguing with Olga, about my quest to have all conversations at home in English.

One day as I came home from work, I found Olga speaking Spanish, and it bothered me.

"I don't want to hear another word in this house, unless it's in English," I said at the top of my lungs. "Now we are all Americans, we are in the United States, and everybody here has to speak English," I added.

Of course, Olga did not stay silent, and reacted with annoyance because she wanted to keep on using Spanish.

Eventually we reached an agreement but it was clear that we, as a family, had to make an effort to integrate into the new country that welcomed us with generosity.

However, family life reverted to its Cuban origins on Sundays. Olga enjoyed enormously cooking the plentiful breakfasts and lunches that filled our table, and had nothing to do with American cuisine but a lot of those Cuban and Spanish dishes that I have always loved.

Ed, Gus older brother, parents Elia and Eduardo, and Gus in the patio of the family home in Hialeah. Elia and Eduardo often visited Gus before Fidel Castro seized power in Cuba.

Selling used cars in Cuba

During the summer vacations our kids travelled to Cuba, where they stayed with their maternal grandparents, Roberto and Elena, absorbing the deep family affection and the Cuban lifestyle.

From Havana they went to Cienfuegos and enjoyed the provincial life with my parents, an experience so emotion filled for them that after returning home it was difficult for them to readapt to Miami for the new school year.

Havana in 1957, when Gus Machado started his business selling used cars.

Meanwhile, I did not stop working in Miami to provide support.

I remember that around that time I was contacted by a group of Cubans who had heard of me and my budding used car sales from the Sinclair gas station.

The men, who travelled from Cuba looking for used cars to take them to the island, came to my business asking me to accompany them to auctions, and help them as guide and translator.

Until then I used to sell only those cars that were brought to my store, but I was not acquainted with used vehicle auctions.

After making their purchases, they drove the vehicles to Key West, a long six hour drive, and from there they took the ferry shuttling to Havana.

If you took one car on the ferry, the round trip was $60. If you took two, it was $120, and so on. To me that looked like a great deal, and that was how I became interested in the business of taking used cars to Cuba.

Selling used cars in Cuba reconfirmed in me the great opportunities available for my business career in that flourishing trade. "After all," I thought, "cars are a basic necessity and there will always be a market for them."

I wasn't wrong.

Then, Castro's Revolution

During all of 1958 business was, literally, rolling. I was sending a car per week to Cuba in the last few months of that year, and in Miami the sales were also flourishing.

The greatest demand for cars in Cuba was for Chevrolets. All Chevy models were selling like hot cakes. Another car make that was very popular was the Studebaker, which had more sporty models.

In December, there were rumors that the guerrillas were heading to Havana. By then 80 percent of the Cuban population opposed Batista's government. Even though it was a heavy-handed and unpopular government, it allowed a normal business climate, and more so with the United States.

But even then, there were people already warning of the communist tendencies of the Sierra Maestra rebels.

Gus Machado often traveled on this ferry between Key West and Havana for his used car trade business.

However, the majority did not seem overly concerned, and quite the opposite, had a positive outlook on the Castroite guerrillas supposedly fighting for an ideal of liberty and justice.

So, on January 1959, we received the news that Batista had fled on New Year's Eve, and the *barbudos* (bearded ones) were approaching on the long march to the capital.

Things did not change much in the first months of the year. I kept on shipping used cars to Havana as usual. In Cuba there was a pervasive atmosphere of euphoria about what the people believed was a liberation from the Batista dictatorship.

For entrepreneurs like me, instead, the most important thing was to know how the new government would behave regarding facilities and/or regulations affecting commercial activities in general, and for imports in particular.

Nobody at that time could imagine what was about to be imposed. But the first signals didn't take long to appear.

Scarcely a week after coming to power in January the revolutionary government announced that it was going to govern by decree for the following 18 months.

In Miami the news from Havana was booming. One of them was about the violent entrance of the Castroite guerrillas into the four biggest casinos operating in the capital, and smashing the slot machines with sledge hammers.

A Sunday family visit to Gus's new dealership (Star Motors) in the early 60s. The children were treated to a coke from the soda machine. The four children in the front are Rudy, Robert, Myra and Lydia, holding Cokes. Olga and Gus are standing behind the kids. Also in the picture the family of Lydia's godparents and relatives visiting from Cuba.

A View of Havana's presidential palace in 1958, a year before Fidel Castro's takeover. Gus Machado stopped doing business in Cuba because of the Communist regime.

In May 1959, the Agrarian Reform Law was enacted, ordering the confiscation of all properties exceeding 400 hectares in order to give them to the farmers. It was the coming of new revolutionary justice that began to generate nervousness among the Cuban entrepreneurs.

My parents' and grandparents' lands in Cienfuegos did not reach that size, but it wasn't difficult to foresee that further confiscations would be issued and nothing could be done about it.

Doors closed to me by the dictatorship

In the mean time, I kept sending cars from Miami because demands gave no signals of diminishing.

Cars were selling well, and there were even people buying them to resell, which was also a good deal.

The importation procedures had not changed, but the economy was no longer the same.

The great flow of tourists and the intense activity in the casinos, bringing a considerable amount of money to the island, began to diminish especially due to the radical measures of the Castro regime, which included bloody executions by firing squads after summary trials of those accused of being counter-revolutionaries.

The Ferry that Gus used to shuttle between Florida and Cuba in the late 1950s, disappeared upon Fidel Castro's arrival.

By mid 1960, there were rumors that the United States was planning a commercial embargo against the regime of Fidel Castro, who was already showing signs of being an autocratic and fractious leader.

Worried because an embargo would mean the end of my business in Cuba, I travelled to Havana in order to solve and close pending deals.

As of my arrival the atmosphere was bizarre. The vast militarization of the city was obvious, and you could feel that fear was in the air.

Right away I went to see a customer who still owed the final payment on a car he had bought from me.

I clearly remember going to the bank to cash the check, and since the Cuban pesos would be worthless in Miami, I exchanged them for dollars and wrapped up my return trip.

"This is the last check I'll be able to collect in Cuba," I thought.

A few days later, in October 1960, the U.S. government prohibited all business transactions with Cuba, except those for food and medications. My business venture selling used cars in the island had come to an end.

Fortunately, I was able to cash that last check. But what seemed like a frustrating experience gave way to new business opportunities.

6

New Horizons (1961-63)

After cashing that check just in time before the economic sanctions against Castro's Cuba went into effect, I left island and never returned.

At that point the moods were heated, and uncertainty was rampant. While the summary trials and firing squads were chomping away, the Castro regime was turning more cruel and radical, persecuting and jailing everyone who disagreed.

To me, who had never bothered with politics, that situation was a wake up call, and from then on I became fully aware of the need to fight for freedom in Cuba.

But all that would come later. For the time being my concern was the well-being of our relatives, Olga's and mine, as communism advanced in Cuba.

Many Cubans decided to send their children abroad first, in that great plan organized by the Catholic Church in Miami, known as Operation Peter Pan. Later, the exodus became massive, mainly to the United States, but also to other countries like Mexico and Venezuela.

Many in Cuba were deluded by the idea that it would be just a matter of months before the socialist experiment collapsed, and the return to the previous status would be a lot sooner than expected.

Then came the attempted invasion on April 1961, and its failure, by the lack of full support from President John F. Kennedy, convinced many more that the time had come to leave the island.

However, regardless of what was going on after Castro took over, many families remained firm on their decision not to abandon their country. Among those were my parents and Olga's parents.

However, foreseeing what could happen as a result of Fidel Castro's outrageous decisions, my parents in Cienfuegos were getting ready to move to Havana, considering the possibility of leaving behind family properties that maybe they would have to put up for sale in a manner they had never planned.

Fortunately, when Cubans began to arrive in Miami, we already had been here for a decade of presence and work which gave us a great advantage in the midst of the new problems and opportunities emerging in South Florida as a result of the Cuban crisis.

As you can imagine, the advent of communism in Cuba

changed many things not only in my family's situation but also in my career as an entrepreneur.

Expansion of my business in Miami

I continued conducting my used car business from the old gas station in North Miami, but by then I had more experience, had met a lot more people and had a little more money to invest.

That was when I decided to get rid of the gas station and the small shop where I started as a used car dealer, and started looking for a bigger business.

It was at that time that I saw an ad for the auction of a bankrupt used car business.

The garage was named Pure Gas Station, and was located at a corner of Le Jeune Road a NW 7th Street, a busy spot near the airport. Next to that garage was the lot of another used car dealer that had also filed for bankruptcy. The auction for that other place was not for the land but for the dealership, including some 20 or 30 cars.

So I made an offer and ended buying the used car lot. From what I remember most of the cars were a bit old, so I dealt with the Pure Gas Station owners and they leased me the station from month to month. I moved to that new place, where I stayed for almost five years.

There I founded, along with a partner who had shown interest, a used car dealersip named Star Motors, my first business totally dedicated to auto sales.

The agency's location had the advantage of being next to a West Star, a gas station a close to the Miami Airport, which was already a busy hub of international tourism.

Le Jeune Road's active traffic usually attracted customers from all walks of life. The agency began to flourish from the very start, without much need for advertising, and all that was really needed was to treat customers with silk gloves and a broad smile.

In the meantime, we moved to a larger house in West Hialeah, closer to the Palmetto and the school where the kids were going for their elementary education.

I remember that my kids were the only ones in their school who spoke Spanish. At least in that school there were no other Hispanic families. The Cuban wave started much later.

That was in part on account of my insistence on speaking English at home. I was convinced, as I mentioned earlier, that integration to the society where we lived was a key element for success.

On account of that, our life had become more sociable as we became familiar with the city and made new friends.

We were lucky to have neighbors that treated us with great kindness and acceptance, despite our cultural differences.

As far as my work, my daily dynamics had lost no intensity. I say it again and again: I was never scared of working, on the contrary, I've always liked to dedicate all necessary efforts to

Gus with his parents Elia and Eduardo, in his South Miami home.

push a project forward, and more so in those days, when my second business initiative was opening a new horizon for me.

Family vacations in Mexico instead of Cuba

The Cuban situation turned even worse the following year. In February 1962 the embargo by the United States was radicalized to the point of including almost all types of exports to the island.

The worst came months later, in October, when one of the most critical episodes of the Cold War took place: the 13 days that kept the world in suspense, the Cuban Missile Crisis.

It was a moment of great anxiety for us Cubans living in Miami. The media was informing us about a possible confrontation between the United States and the Soviet Union over a Cuban stage.

There was always a hope that the confrontation would build enough tension to force the collapse of Fidel Castro's communist regime. But the crisis passed, Kennedy reached an agreement with the Soviets, and for the time being the dictator managed to survive.

By the time that the Missile Crisis ended there had already been two waves of Cuban exiles, including the 14,000 kids that came in the Peter Pan Operation.

Despite the situation, our parents still had not made up their minds to leave the island. Our kids, who had already shared several vacations with their grandparents in Havana as well as Cienfuegos, were now missing them.

Both Rudy and Myra, who had spent a whole year, before Castro coming to power, at the Cienfuegos family farm, missed my parents and the country life they had with them, filled with adventures for four and five year old children, respectively.

Since the trips between Havana and Miami were limited to bare essentials, and the Cubans were not allowed to travel to American territory, the only way to get together for the families separated by the revolution was to travel to a third country.

That's just what we had to do for our vacations, in order for the children to enjoy the affections of their grandparents, and

Ed, Elia, Eduardo and Gus at the new house he bought for his parents in Hialeah, when they finally decided to leave Cuba, in 1985.

that took place in Mexico City, a place where our parents were allowed to travel.

Those were unforgettable meetings, especially for the children, and particularly for Robert, the youngest one.

When we landed at the airport, I immediately rented a car to see the country, especially the beaches at Acapulco and Veracruz.

Those two weeks meant enjoyment and rest, sharing time with the family and relaxing. I've always liked vacations because besides dedicating time to my family, I had the chance to mull about what was coming ahead, what my immediate future would bring.

New partners and new companies

The Star Motors dealership we set up in Le Jeune was a school for me. I learned many things: the details of choosing the autos we resold, the models exhibit, and the price strategy to compete with other dealers, the secrets of a friendly relationship with costumers, and other gimmicks to increase sales.

The business coincided with the massive arrival of Cubans to Miami, so I started selling used cars to newly arrived Cubans that scantily had $100 in their pockets, and gave them easy weekly payment options that they could afford and defray like clockwork.

After five years business had grown enough and I was selling higher class cars. Then a group of Cuban investors came up with the idea of buying the business from me.

I told them:

"If you want to buy, I accept."

I'll never forget who they were: Alejandro Llanos, Saturnino Conde, the man with the money; Felo Conde, his son; Lucio Well, Oscar Gómez and Napoleón Llanos.

The investors, however, stated that they would buy the business, for a good amount of money by the way, but on one condition:

"We want you to stay in the business with us," they proposed.

Finally I accepted and we became partners for the next five years. After that, with the incoming capital, everything improved, car purchasing was much better and we increased the sales.

Later I found a promising place on Southwest 27th Avenue and 8th Street, in what is presently known as the entrance to Little Havana, and I opened American Auto Sales, a new business in which I controlled everything, without partners.

By then I considered myself a bit more mature as an entrepreneur, and I felt more secure when it came to taking calculated business risks.

The place was well located. It was midway between Coral Gables and Coconut Grove, and had an entrance on 27th Avenue, which connected the north and south of Miami.

Traffic was incredible and the public had a chance to see the showroom from the street when driving along that avenue. Quite a few used to drop by and check the details of the vehicles for sale.

Sales were so plentiful that there was an opportunity for more growth. I thought that opening a new dealership could double sales thus multiplying my profits.

I didn't think twice about it and contacted two Cubans who would be the second set of partners with whom I had a business relationship: my good friends Jaime Rosumoski and Pepe Valle.

We agreed to join as partners for a new business in another busy Miami street: 8th Street and Le Jeune Road.

After giving up American Auto Sales, I made a partnership with a second used car agency that we called Big Trail Auto.

By this time, Miami was becoming the Mecca of Cuban exiles. Tens of thousands of compatriots, already convinced that the return to the island was no way near, were pouring their energy into the creation of opportunities to make money.

Of course, the growing exile population meant the overnight addition of a clientele that no one had expected. Every exile was a potential buyer, especially because used cars were cheaper and indispensable to move around in a city that was growing by the day.

The marvels of family life

My son Rudy missed the art sessions with his grandfather Pepe, who sculpted gargoyles and lions to decorate buildings in Havana. So, he jumped with joy when he found out that his maternal grandparents, the parents of my wife Olga, had finally decided to come to exile in Miami.

My in-laws Pepe and Lola arrived towards the end of 1962 and settled in Miami Beach, which in those days was not the glamorous and trendy place it is today, but rather a quiet neighborhood for retirees, older people and low-income families.

The apartment they chose to move into was three blocks away from the beach, so not only was it a blessing for the kids to share time with their grandparents, but an obsession for going to the beach.

I was working six days a week then, from very early in the

morning until well into the night, so I didn't have a lot of time to share with my family. That's why Sundays became the day to celebrate, to share the intimacy of a meal, or splashing on the ocean.

Each Sunday was an occasion to forget about the daily pressures of business and concentrate on the emotions of being a normal family guy, with joy and without distractions of any type.

I've always liked to cultivate the jovial side of my personality, cracking jokes and laughing. I've never liked the attitude of "I'm the boss," "do as I say," and my children know that better than anyone.

For me it was important to impart values to my kids: joy, hope, putting a lot of energy into whatever had to be done, and always having the time to laugh out loud with a good joke.

7

Family, Business and Opportunities (1964-70)

When 1964 came around, the country was beginning to get over and assimilate from the commotion created by the assassination of President John F. Kennedy. The event had become a national trauma, also for the Cuban exile, since there were rumors everywhere that Fidel Castro was suspected of being one of the instigators.

Shortly afterwards it came out that the assassin, Lee Harvey Oswald, had been in contact with officials of the Cuban dictatorship in Mexico before the assassination, thus fueling all sort of conspiracy theories.

But at that time I was not focused on national or international politics, just bent on strongly promoting the sales at my used car business.

At the time I wanted to make a name for myself, so people would say that buying a car from Gus Machado was the best

Gus Machado in an advertising campaign during the 1985 Carnival.

thing they could do.

With each passing day I understood better that the essential part for success in any business was to present a good image. A good image, of course, was related to order, cleanliness, honesty and keeping your word of honor.

In those times the pledged word had a supreme value. That word and a handshake was enough to close a deal or agree to an investment. Breaking that simple rule meant being excluded from the business community, and guaranteed the stigma of a bad reputation that was very difficult to wash away.

Having a good reputation meant more opportunities for you, in an economy that was beginning to bloom, with inflation at a low level.

The dollar as currency was even stronger than it is today, and the economy was expanding, thanks to a number of measures taken by the late President Kennedy, of which the most important was a reduction of tax rates, personal and corporative.

This generated a prosperity benefitting especially the American middle class. For me those good tidings meant that people had money in their pockets, and therefore buying a car was one of their main options.

Additionally, in Florida the economy was getting a boost from the massive flow of Cubans escaping the plague of revolution in Cuba, and bringing their assets, inventiveness and capacity for work.

All that was reflected on the sales, which began growing slowly but steadily, in good part thanks to the enthusiastic immigrants for whom a used vehicle was the first step to a promising future in Uncle Sam's land.

New destination for business: Puerto Rico

In the middle of that environment, I considered all possible opportunities to take advantage of the economic situation.

I remembered the frustration I had felt for not being able

GUS MACHADO'S AMERICAN DREAM, MEMOIRS | 77

Gus Machado was an accomplished master in the art of advertising, a skill that helped him to become the greatest car salesman for the Hispanic market nationwide in the 1980s.

to continue exporting vehicles to Cuba, thanks to the coming of Castroism and the ending of business opportunities on the island. A business that had rendered me good profits.

But I told myself: "Cuba is not the only place for me to export cars."

I didn't know, back then, anyone who lived in any country other than Cuba, except for one place: Puerto Rico.

I had met many Puerto Rican friends who came to Florida after 1953, during the biggest migration out of the *Isla del Encanto*, when I was settling down in Joliet.

In 1964 Puerto Rico had been for 12 years an Associated State in agreement with the United States, which allowed its own government and Constitution. The economy had changed noticeably from mainly large sugar cane plantations to manufacturing industries.

For me that translated into: more work, more money, and more markets for my used cars.

I thought: "It's a gold mine; few in Miami are taking advantage of that market, few speak Spanish around here like I do, and they need vehicles."

In a brief time I expedited the process of exporting used vehicles to Puerto Rico, and thus was born the appreciation I have for that island, which has given me not only great friends but many satisfied customers over the years.

It was while exporting automobiles to Puerto Rico that my life began to take flight.

I would buy a parcel of used cars in the best possible conditions using my company American Auto Sales at Le Jeune Road, and then prepared them for exporting to Puerto Rico.

In those days there was a preference for cars made by General Motors. The island was opening to tourism and investors, and the large number of factories, especially textile manufacturers opening all over the place was noteworthy.

The process was not complicated, so in less time that I had thought I began to send a small number of automobiles every week to Puerto Rico from the Port of Miami.

Business was very good, although limited, since I could only sell a determined number of cars per month, because competition had started.

I travelled several times to San Juan because I had to negotiate with the resellers and owners of auto agencies, who were shrewd at haggling for discounts. For me the important thing was to establish a reliable network of distributors that would open the options for larger deals in the future.

My parents in Miami Beach

In Miami business marched at a steady pace, but the Cuban situation always made me feel uneasy. Cubans kept fleeing, by all imaginable means, from the abuses and persecution by Castro's dictatorship, which had already declared itself openly communist.

The topic of the dictatorship never ceased to frustrate me, especially because my family, still living in Havana, kept us aware of the excesses of Castroism and the ravages of shortages.

We could still rely on those trips to Mexico as the only way to see my parents, thinking especially about our kids, because we had the conviction that we should strengthen family ties.

But I tried to convince them that it was time to leave Cuba

to join us in Miami, and finally my parents accepted the idea of getting away from the kind of life they were enduring.

Miami, and particularly Miami Beach, was beginning to enjoy the status of a tourism and showbusiness capital.

One of the best known celebrities was the comedian Jackie Gleason, whose shows at the Fillmore Theater were very popular. Gleason was a golf fan, an activity I would pursue years later as a zealous member of the Miami Beach Golf Club.

Miami Beach was also the set in 1964 for the historic presentation of the Beatles, when they came to United States for the first time, to appear on the Ed Sullivan Show and were an immediate sensation in all their ensuing appearances.

Certainly, the Ed Sullivan Show was one of my favorite programs, and I admit that watching it taught me a lot for my future media adventures.

I don't know if it was for those showbiz reasons or just the proximity to the beach, but when my parents came from Cuba sometime later, they also chose to settle in Miami Beach, and that had a positive impact for our family, especially for the children, who were thrilled to spend time with their grandparents.

Life in Miami Beach was very dynamic. We were able to appreciate that on our Sunday walks around the South Beach area, presided on by the imposing presence of the Fontainebleau Hotel, and other Art Deco buildings such as the Eden Roc, Deauville and Carrillon.

A common sight in that area was the Cadillac convertibles lugging glamorous people. It made me think of selling luxury cars like that to my customers on Le Jeune Road and Puerto Rico.

The Sixties, a great decade for business

The Sixties were definitely a great decade. There was a lot of turbulence on the streets due to the civil rights protests. But in Miami we had a different life rhythm that was perhaps more influenced by tourism and the fun-loving people on vacations and those who came to stay, bringing money and prosperity.

A brand-new car could be bought for $2,650, about a third of the average family's annual income. But a used car in good

conditions, like the ones I sold, could be bought for a lot less.

For anyone who had the will and energy to find a decent job, there were many options. A person who went out job-hunting in the morning could start working in the afternoon and be earning money right away.

Gas was no problem: the gallon of regular fuel was going for 32 cents. The automobile market was essentially American makes, as the current invasion of Japanese and Korean cars was still a decade away.

The best-selling vehicles were always one of the four brands that dominated the market: General Motors, Ford, Chrysler and American Motors. Detroit was the great Mecca to visit at least once a year to keep up with the trends.

In 1964 the market went through the roof when Ford launched its Mustang, the first of the so-called *muscle cars* to reach great popularity, especially among young customers.

Between 1964 and 1966, four models changed the trends of the American car market: the Pontiac Tempest GTO and the Firebird, the Chevrolet Camaro and the Dodge Challenger. These vehicles had in common a relatively small chassis but a powerful engine.

By 1968, when the riots against the Vietnam War reached a frenzied level, sales were booming at American Auto Sales, not only in the local market but in exports to Puerto Rico as well.

Barely a year before, the island's majority had voted in a referendum to keep the Associated Free State status. Only one percent of the voters considered that Puerto Rico should become independent of the United States, a crushing defeat for the *independentistas*.

Looking at that stage in retrospective, I would say that it was an era of consolidation for my business. Out of American Auto Sales, I founded Big Trail in 1969, completely independent and ready to face the new challenges.

By the end of that decade, marked by the elation generated by the Moon Landing in 1969, and the beginning of that special era, I went ahead with my new business and ideas bubbling in my head.

Family life in Miami Beach

Despite all the excitement surrounding my life as a businessman, I always had time for family meetings.

The maternal grandparents' tiny apartment on Miami Beach remained a meeting spot. My father-in-law, Pepe, a man with an impressive work ethic, had found a job in Hialeah, so every weekday he drove the used car I got for him so he could take care of his responsibilities in terms of sculptures and art.

I always tried to have a joyful and enjoying relationship with my kids. I treated all of them the same way, with the same love and attention.

My daughter Myra used to say that I always tried to solve their problems, no matter what they were. She was right on target. I've always liked to help those who need it, and if it meant anyone in my family even more so. Family should always be the priority.

But beyond problems and work, I always had time for fun.

One time, I went out to buy some percussion instruments, a bongo drum and claves, and went home to surprise the kids.

After arriving, I play a vinyl of Cuban music on the record player, and showed them the instruments trying to show them how to play them. I was trying to teach them a bit of Cuban rhythm, because I've always loved music and dancing. Dancing and singing have always been one of my preferences because they are ways of spreading joy and optimism, two values with which I identify myself deeply.

Of course, in Hialeah we lived surrounded by good neighbors, but they neither spoke Spanish nor knew our culture. And in Miami Beach, where the grandparents lived, the majority of the neighbors were retired Jews who had come here to spend the last years of their lives.

Sundays were special days when the kids were still kids and had not grown up yet.

At times I used to take Rudy fishing. My son always loved the sea and watching the ships come and go along the Miami Beach canals.

I remember that there was always a good breakfast of eggs, bacon, coffee and Cuban bread. But the best part was the *almuerzos* at the grandparents. Always a Spanish omelette, grilled shrimps, fresh fish and seafood stew.

Family life, not only in that time but in all the times that came later, was always one of the key ingredients of my professional success. The reason why I became what is commonly called a work addict, or *workaholic*, was because I wanted to propel my family ahead. My dedication to business was always motivated by my wish to give stability and a future for my children. However, the constant challenges of work open unexpected pathways that at the same time are positive opportunities, but also present risks. And that's because there are no good opportunities without risk.

8

An explosive decade (1970-1979)

The advent of a new decade brought with it several novelties in all my life's tracks up to that point. Twenty years had gone by since I first stepped on American soil, in the now distant year of 1949, when I was sent by my parents to a military school in North Carolina.

A lot of water had passed under the bridge. By now I had been able to consolidate myself as an entrepreneur, had my own business, and was in the process of expanding my market not only in Miami but in Puerto Rico as well.

I was buying used cars in Miami, all classes and models, and selling them to all the dealers on the island, with excellent results. Sometimes in a single order I would send as many as 100 cars to my clients in Puerto Rico.

But the sales were beginning to run into a series of external obstacles about which little could be done.

Gus Machado during the recording of a commercial to promote his car dealership.

The '70s began with many changes in all ways of life nationwide, and in particular a great assortment of new car models directed at a younger public whose power as consumers was awakening.

Automobiles like the Camaro and the Mustang had proven their popularity during the second half of the '60s, but in the '70s things turned more complicated.

It was the heyday of demonstrations against the Vietnam War and the hippy movement. For the Cubans in Miami, it was the eternal struggle against communism in Cuba but also for assimilating to the new nation that embraced them as refugees.

During that period, besides Gus Machado, other entrepreneurs were also making a name for themselves in the business community. One of them was Manuel Capó, founder of the renowned El Dorado Furniture, whose arrival in 1966 was an adventure worthy of an action movie.

Capó and his family named the store El Dorado in honor of the tiny vessel on which they sailed to escape Castroism, braving the treacherous waters of the Florida Strait, on their way to Mexico, and from there to Miami.

Another prominent entrepreneur opened a restaurant in Miami that eventually became an icon of the Cuban-American culture. He was the late Felipe Valls and the restaurant was *Versailles*, which opened its doors in 1971.

Felipe's history is very similar to mine, although with a few variations. Like me, he came to study in a military school in the United States, in his case it was the Riverside Military Academy, of Gainesville, Georgia, in 1947 –two years before I entered the Edwards Academy in North Carolina.

Afterwards he returned to Cuba in 1950, and worked as an entrepreneur until, forced by the Castroist dictatorship, he came to Miami to pursue his professional career.

These personal stories -mine, Manuel Capó's and Felipe Valls', among those of many other successful Cubans- demonstrate that there were opportunities for anyone with the firm conviction to work hard and persistently.

Radical changes in the '70s

At the beginning of the decade, for reasons that are not easy to explain, tourism crashed. The "Magic City" that had been a paradise for visitors, mainly from Latin America, little by little crumpled down into a place that was losing its former glamour.

Tourists, instead, began heading massively to a new destination more appetizing than Miami: Disney World, which opened its doors in 1971 and immediately became a magnet for international tourists that used to come to South Florida.

The "Miami" brand, the "World Capital for Fun," suffered a severe damage in 1972, when the two leading political parties -Democratic and Republican-, chose Miami Beach for their respective conventions.

Both political events, within the framework of that year's presidential election, which Richard Nixon eventually won, were a public relations disaster, due to the violent demonstrations that erupted.

I remember those demonstrations. Groups of young people were moving all over Miami Beach raising hell. Any reason, silly or not, was deemed good to spark a protest, and most people felt threatened.

Lacking the money flow that came with tourism, Orlando's competition for the visitors' dollars, and the negative impact of the political violence, the economy was affected to the point of hurting used cars sales, and that was my main business.

The City of Hialeah approved the naming of a street dedicated to Gus Machado, in celebration of his more than 40 years as the city's most iconic businessman.

That situation reached a boiling point in 1973 with the infamous oil embargo against the United States, as a result of the ongoing Middle East conflict, which caused a terrible fuel shortage, sent the prices through the roof and unleashed one of the worst economic crisis in the history of this country.

Until then, everything had been rose colored, but things began to change dramatically, and we had to adapt to the changes.

Separation of the family and dedication to work

Inside our family the situation was not less complicated. Due to many factors happening during my time of business consolidation, by the end of the '60s, my family life took a radical turn.

In 1969, after a bit less than 20 years of marriage, Olga and I separated, I undertook a new status alone, and this made me see things differently.

The children remained with their mother during those years, and stayed focused on their studies. As it could be expected, the separation influenced everything.

The ending of married life had its highs and lows. I missed the daily family life and the Sundays, when we would all get together to enjoy a good meal and watch my favorite TV programs, like The High Chaparral and Bonanza, and Walt Disney's program which was the kids' favorite.

I missed Olga's Spanish omelettes and the short fishing trips with my son Rudy in Miami Beach.

But at the same time I accepted the reality that I had to get even more involved in my business to make it grow.

I was never afraid of the possibility of living alone. I had that experience when I came to study in a North Carolina military school, at the early age of 16.

Additionally, my cheerful and sociable temperament and my good humor, which never left me during all my life, helped me in this new stage of my life.

My main concern was my family's welfare. I always wanted to remain available to help my kids solve any problem that came up. As natural, Olga kept the house and went on living there with our four children, who were still in school. And my life continued as before: work, work and more work.

"Dad is a *workaholic*," my own daughter Myra would say afterwards. She was far from wrong.

Occasionally, Rudy would accompany me at work, and helped me cleaning the cars for sale or moving them around from one place to another. In summer, Rudy worked at the gas station next to Big Trail Used Cars, which was the name of my company then, on Le Jeune Road.

I was trying to teach him the work ethics and the importance of learning to produce his own income without waiting for anyone to put money in his hands.

In 1969, when he turned 15 and was able to get his own driver's license, Rudy was able to buy, with his own money, his own car: a used 1962 Corvette, the fashionable car among the young, and he paid $100 for it.

Sometimes I would invite Rudy's friends to help moving used vehicles I had bought, to drive them in caravan to the Port of Miami, destined to Puerto Rico. The kids, who had recently received their restricted licenses, were excited by the task.

It didn't take long for me to force Rudy to sell the blessed Corvette because he was getting into a lot of problems racing

Gus Machado dancing with his daughter Myra on her wedding day, Miami, August 9, 1975.

in illegal competitions. We sold it to an officer of the Hialeah motorcycle police.

My daughter Myra, the oldest one, who was already 18, had graduated from high school and was taking her second year at Miami Dade Community College.

Sometime later she decided to follow her mother who had moved to a place in the outskirts of Gainesville, in North Florida, restart her life with my son Robert.

Myra had made up her mind to be self-sufficient and take charge of her future, so she returned to Miami to get married after finishing the two years of college and began to earn her own

Gus Machado with his sons and family during an anniversary celebration in 1986.

income. Later she went back to school at Florida International University (FIU), where she studied for three more years until she graduated in 1977 with a degree in Special Education.

For Myra it was very important to follow her vocation and she worked educating special needs children for the next 35 years, something that earned my admiration and respect.

Rudy, like a spirited steed, also went on to find his own path and married a Hialeah girl with whom he had a son. Family responsabilities, like it was in my case, led him drop out of school to provide support.

But the youth of both Rudy and his wife contributed to their separation and he decided to move north, near Gainesville, where Olga, Roberto and Myra were living. There he finally found peace of mind in the Ocala countryside, which reminded him of the family farm in Cienfuegos, where he had spent many happy times during his childhood, there he went on with his life, marrying again and raising a family.

Despite the diversity of paths that took the family after the separation, I was always there to attend any needs of my children. Because, like my daughter Myra would say, I love to listen to and to help to take care of the needs of others, and seeing the happy endings.

Oil crisis in the '70s and new business opportunities

The oil embargo by the Arab members of the Organization of Petroleum Exporting Countries (OPEC) against the United States, for supporting Israel during the Yom Kippur War, had an impact on many aspects of American life, particularly on the auto industry.

The long lines in the gas stations all over the country, due to the shortages caused by the embargo traumatized many consumers and caused a major concern for the car sales companies.

All of a sudden, people become aware of the fuel's value. Many persons cut down their use of motor vehicles and started riding bicycles more often in order to save gas. Many vacation

Gus Machado addresses the public during the Gus Machado Way's dedication, in June 2012. Also present at the event: Miami's Mayor Tomás Regalado.

trips were cancelled that year and the next. All activities that involved traveling by car were limited to a bare minimum.

When the cost of electricity reflected the inflation resulting from the high costs of fuel, people started taking all kinds of shortcuts. Some installed insulation panels to block heat and keep the nights' cooler temperature inside their houses, in order to save energy. Others restricted their use of air conditioning by using ceilings fans.

And then labor conflicts began at the Detroit car

Gus during the filming of his weekly program at Gus Machado Ford's headquarters in 1984.

manufacturers, thus bringing a drop in the production of American vehicles. When that happened I reversed my business strategy in Puerto Rico. I started buying cars on the island and bringing them to Miami.

At the time, Asian cars, like Toyota, Datsun and Nissan, gained popularity in the American market since these were smaller and more gas-efficient, like the Toyota Corolla and many others.

Toyota had sold its first Corolla in the American market in 1966, but six years later, in 1972, it was number one of all the imported cars sold in the United States, with sales reaching a million units.

For some time I sold those models and I introduced the Isuzu to Miami, a brand previously unknown here and they became very popular.

That was when I had an opportunity that channeled me in a much more promising direction.

New car business on the island

The way I managed to reach an agreement with General Motors was very interesting and it is a good example of how complicated it was to sell new cars, in comparison to used ones.

In 1974, when I couldn't even imagine becoming formally a seller of new cars, a situation arose in Puerto Rico that was completely unexpected for me.

I was selling used cars on the island, while the new ones were sold by the main distributor over there, Caribe Motors, which supplied all the car sellers in Puerto Rico.

Caribe Motors had a contract with General Motors for the distribution of new autos. But they began to have problems at that moment because there was no demand for many of the cars they had bought to distribute, and they lacked the necessary insight to determine the public's preference and demand.

Unsold cars began to pile up at Caribe Motors to the point that by mid- year they could no longer stay in business and filed

Gus Machado often turned his showroom into a television studio to promote his vehicles, a pioneer at the time.

for bankruptcy.

The demise of Caribe Motors orphaned all the dealers that depended on that company to distribute new cars.

Then I started getting calls from dealers that were upset and desperate because they had no new cars to sell, despite the demand.

I sold them used cars, but they wanted new ones, so I seized the opportunity, although not without difficulties.

I did my own research on how to export new autos from Miami to the island, and looked for a financially viable example that I could deal with.

I started by asking the Puerto Rican dealers about the type of cars they needed. Then I dealt with the already established General Motors dealers in Miami to bring them the orders from my customers in Puerto Rico.

There were at the time three dealers: Anthony Abraham, Don Allen Chevrolet, and Sark Chevrolet. Those were the three sources I would go to place the orders from my Puerto Rican customers.

For example, I would go to Puerto Rico and ask the customer: "What car do you need?" and they would answer: "I need a Malibu, or a Montecarlo." I would take the order, and then check that the customer had a credit line open at Citibank, the financier, to cover the cost of the order.

Then I went to a Citibank in Miami, explain to the manager that a customer like, let's say Rossi Motors –a large General Motors distributor in Puerto Rico–, had given me an order for 4 or 5 Montecarlos, and 3 or 4 Malibus. Then the manager checked the financial aspect and authorized the order, at that point I was able to collect.

That way, after building a working relationship with customers and the bank, I started the operation. Once the order was placed, the cars arrived in something like 4 or 6 weeks, and then I prepared them, took them to the dock and passed them through customs.

Of course, I paid taxes and fees for each car, as required for exportation, because the bank required it. But once I had taken the car to the port, I collected my profit from the bank.

That's when I set up the company GM Motors Exports, and started making some very good deals for about a little less than two years.

Sales on the island received a crucial financial boost when the IRS in Washington approved Section 936, exempting American companies established in Puerto Rico to paying federal taxes on their profits.

It was a moment of an incredible economic expansion in which more than 100,000 jobs were created and, of course, increased the sales of new cars tremendously. It was a perfect time for large deals and making many new friends on the island, thus laying the foundations for a full- fledged position in the automobile market.

One thing was to sell used cars and sell them as best I could, and a totally different thing was offering the public the latest models, with all the advertising fanfare that preceded those sales, all of which opened my eyes to a universe I had not seen before.

Friends and golf in Puerto Rico

Another line of business that prospered during my years of activities in Puerto Rico was leasing cars, a concept that was rather new on the island at the time.

Throughout my years of doing business in Puerto Rico I ran into many persons who showed me their quality as human beings. I don't want to omit mentioning the relationships and friendships I found and cultivated during those years of activity in Puerto Rico.

There I met Gloria in the late '70s, my wife for several years. I also met many personalities and friends that had a positive influence on me.

Among those was my friend Héctor González, a dynamic Puerto Rican who was highly successful in the car rental business, so much so that he flew on his own private plane. Héctor and I worked together on very profitable deals.

In Puerto Rico I met a well-known Cuban, who had become famous on the island, where he arrived after a journey, leaving Cuba in 1960 to New York and from there to San Juan.

I mean my good friend Guillermo Álvarez-Guédez, a peerless comedian with whom I spent a lot of time on the island and later in Miami, where he came to live and to solidify his fame a genial humorist.

Never have I forgotten his advice that could sound like an exaggeration but was intrinsically wise: "You got to make a joke about everything." For me it meant: "You got to take life with humor and relax."

Another person worthy of great esteem was my good friend Cándido González, whose doubtless merit was initiating me in the mysteries and passion for golf.

Until that time I had considered golf a foolish sport, hardly involving any physical effort. And then, one day my friend

Cándido challenged me:

"I'll give a hundred bucks if you hit the ball with a club at the first swing." We went to a golf course and there I realized how wrong I was: It was really difficult for me to hit the ball.

But after that, thanks to Cándido's patience, I learned to play and from that moment on I was hooked.

I had no idea how important playing golf would be for my business life. For that, I owe my thanks to Cándido.

9

In the Major Leagues (1980-1987)

My new experience selling new cars, instead of used ones, made me understand the capital importance that advertising had for increasing sales.

Until then we had relied on the traditional newspaper ads, and advertising on radio stations including some minor TV campaigns, and these had efficient results.

But with the advent of the new decade, competition became much fiercer. The new dealers were offering competitive specials each week trying to attract a market that had become active, in good part, due to the great money flow that was entering Miami in those years.

The city had undergone many changes since the late '70s. After the anti- Vietnam War demonstrations came the resignation of President Richard Nixon due to the Watergate scandal; and after that the United States had two presidents –

Gus Machado was a tireless golfer, and organized several golf tournaments that marked an era in South Florida.

Gerald Ford and Jimmy Carter– but there seemed to be no end in sight to the many problems lurking from every corner.

But at the same time, people kept up their hopes for a promising future. And nothing better to keep up the spirits than buying a brand new car, to get that feeling of cruising on the right road to prosperity.

That was the prevailing mood, and I was ready to cater to that demand on the buyers market.

Unlike the years of fuel shortages in the early '70s, the

demand for luxury cars was sky-high in the '80s. People were looking for vehicles with big engines and comfort levels beyond anything known before then, such as sophisticated sound systems, power seats and wood and leather trims.

And here is where entrepreneurs like me come into the picture, to offer the best conditions and services for acquiring that longed for new vehicle. And with the new things that were happening, a whole bunch of ideas began to flutter in my head.

New connections with Buick and GM

For my good fortune, my relationship with Buick grew at a fast pace for that economy. Sales were so good that in 1982 I reached an agreement to buy the Seipp Buick dealership operating in Hialeah and to sell Buick cars in South Florida.

The purchase of that dealership went like this:

At the time the economy had been critical, due to several decisions made by the administration of President Jimmy Carter, which jacked up the interest rates to a whopping 20 percent.

This situation hurt many debt-ridden businesses and entrepreneurs; among them a car dealer named John Seipp, who was forced to sell his business.

Seipp had placed anonymously, through a broker, a newspaper ad offering his dealership for sale, but without identifying where in Florida it was located.

I was interested by the offer so I called the broker who was

The golf tournaments organized by Gus Machado since 1985 helped raise hundreds of thousands of dollars for charitable causes.

representing the entrepreneur, to inquire the whereabouts of the business. He refused to reveal the location, unless I signed a confidentiality contract, and gave him an initial deposit.

Practically blind I took the initiative. Signed the contract and paid the deposit. The big surprise came when the broker told me that the dealership was in Hialeah, of all places!

I couldn't believe it, it was like a miracle. I had thought that the location in Florida was outside Miami. So I negotiated a better price, and bought Seipp Buick, the first agency I had for distributing General Motors cars.

The agency was located on 49th Street and 16th Avenue, in Hialeah, on a lot that was also included in the negotiation and that would eventually be extremely useful for my future business.

The contract for selling Buick cars was like a crowning of my efforts in sales after many years of working and learning the market. It was my first formal new car sales dealership, so I decided to do something that proved very convenient: for the first time I used my own name to name the business.

Thus was born Gus Machado Buick & GM, which became one of the most famous dealerships in Miami.

It was my sixth company since I acquired in 1956 that small gas station on Miami Avenue and 17th Street, in the NorthWest, where I began, by accident, to sell used cars.

After that came Star Motors Inc., on Le Jeune Road and 7th Street in Northwest Miami; American Auto Sales, near Little Havana; Big Trail Auto Sales, and GM Auto Export, through

Gus Machado founded important golf events in South Florida, including the Golf Shoot Out in the Doral Eastern Open, the PGA's Senior Golf Classic and the Gus Machado Classic Charity Golf Tournament, in benefit of the American Cancer Society.

which I sold countless vehicles in Puerto Rico.

It was the first time one of my children joined me in the business: my daughter Lydia, who until the present continues with these same responsibilities. Before, my son Rudy had helped me when I was selling used cars in Puerto Rico, in the late '60s and early '70s, but never worked as an employee or executive, since he had other interests and experiences before him.

Also in that time I was accompanied by my dear brother Eduardo, who had established himself in Miami. Ed had a more reserved character than I did, but he was as much, if not more efficient at selling entire fleets of vehicles to government organizations and agencies so that was the sales section that he was in charge of for several years.

The new agency offered me new experiences and great opportunities to grow as a major car seller in the region, in great part due to the success of the brand I was selling.

Buick & GM always offered very attractive and American made models, which cornered a significant part of the consumers in the face of the growing invasion of Japanese and German cars.

One of the best-sellers was the Buick Riviera, which was not cheap in those days (a bit under $12,000) but was a great vehicle. The most luxurious model had reclining leather front seats, power windows and autopilot. I loved that car model so much that it was easy for me to convince the interested customers.

I used a combination of good humor to create a trusting relationship with the customer, to make him/her feel the personal attention.

In fact, I did it so well and so convincingly that sales went up. It was in those moments that the idea emerged forcefully.

The idea was a simple one: I wanted to become the most important promoter for my products. Instead of leaving advertising and promotion in the hands of others, I decided that it was time for me to assume those tasks myself, and use my own image as the main tool.

The idea turned out to be very effective, although it was not entirely new. I had grown up admiring TV programs of the

Gus interviews the famous Puerto Rican golfer Chi Chi Rodríguez.

'50s, especially The Lucy Show, whose leading character, Ricky Ricardo, played by the Cuban actor Desy Arnaz, showed that a Cuban immigrant could succeed in American television, and earn fame and fortune.

On the other hand, throughout my entire career, I had been inspired by a great character that I believe was probably one of the most important car dealers in the history of the United States.

The first time I heard of James Martin Moran, better known as Jim Moran, in '60s, he was in charge of a very famous dealership in his native Chicago, named Midtown Motors.

Jim's history was partly similar to mine. After graduating from high school in 1939, he saved enough money to buy a Sinclair gas station and a few years later he added to it a used car lot, the exact same thing I had done with my gas station in North Miami.

By mid '40s, he was the biggest car seller of the Hudson Company, which later became AMC (American Motors Company). And in 1955, when I was just getting started in Hialeah, Jim was already the largest Ford automobile distributor in the United States.

But for me the most important thing about Jim Moran was that he had been one of the first car sellers to have his own advertising show on TV. He had a great natural talent and great charisma for selling automobiles. He was a great showman whose career had an impact on me.

On one occasion I commented to my wife at the time: "Someday I'm going to be like Jim Moran."

And the moment arrived without my looking for it. After acquiring Seipp Buick and turning it into Gus Machado Buick & GM, I began to think about the advertising strategy to boost sales.

At the time I had a Puerto Rican advertising director, my friend Gabriel Figueroa. I chose him out of several candidates I interviewed to kick-off the agency's advertising campaign.

Gabriel presented a campaign proposal that I liked, so I hired him. We ran the campaign the way we should, how long

During a tournament he sponsored at the Doral Blue Monster, in Florida, Gus interviews the famous Spanish golfer Seve Ballesteros.

it would run, the entries and exits, and the advertising spots for different occasions.

One day, while we were discussing a campaign, Gabriel, who got to know me very well, asked me:

"Gus, why don't you make the commercials?" I replied:

"I? I've never made a commercial in my life."

We went out to dinner to further discuss the idea, and at the end I was convinced that it wasn't a bad proposal after all.

Shortly after, came the decision of making my way in the world of television, showcasing my own advertising spots and applying my charisma as the better sales tools.

I made the first commercial and it was broadcast on

Channel 23 in Miami, which had always been one of the best in the media for reaching the Hispanic community.

The network gave us the less expensive spots on weekends, so I started buying time and running the commercial on the weekends, and the results were terrific.

The first year I had the Buick agency, 82-83, our sales went from $20 millions to $40 millions, meaning that thanks to my commercials, we managed to double car sales and services.

My first steps in the world of advertising

We started filming the first advertising spots right at the agency, and I remember the commotion created when cameras and lights were brought in, as I was rehearsing the script explaining the benefits of our financial packages, and the features of the new models that were coming out.

Having decided to follow Gabriel's suggestion but also relying on my salesman's intuition, which had never failed me, we went ahead. And, of course, I was inspired by the skillful Jim Moran. What I had not imagined was that the stage that was starting in my life, thrusting me into the public scene, not only in Miami but eventually into the highly competitive field of the national automobile trade.

I began to notice the impact of my commercials when my daughter Myra told me one day:

"You are now famous, and I'm proud of you every time

Gus Machado during an event sponsored by his company, next to golf stars Seve Ballesteros, Tom Kite, Lee Trevino and Fred Couples.

you're on TV."

One time Myra reminded me of an anecdote I had forgotten. During a filming session, that was made outdoors, one of the producers signaled to me that I had something on a shoulder.

When I looked, there was indeed something on my right shoulder, a sort of grayish stain. The producer approached napkin in had to clean it: it was a dropping from a bird that just happened to fly by! Of course, I took it as a good luck signal.

We filmed not only inside the agency but in several locations, to add movement and color to the commercials. Sometimes we did it at a marina, with yachts in the background. Other times, we simply filmed on the street, surrounded by a crowd of curious spectators trying to catch a glimpse of the famous Gus Machado making a commercial.

Everywhere I went, restaurants, supermarkets, o simply on the street, people recognized me immediately.

"Gus Machado, what's up," I would hear from people I had never seen before. "Hey, look, that's Gus Machado, the Hialeah businessman," I heard one day as I came in to my friend Felipe Valls' restaurant, Versailles.

Some people even asked me for autographs.

It didn't take long for me to comprehend the importance of televisión for business. And almost immediately doors were opening left and right, something that, I believe, would not have done so otherwise.

The commercials broadcast on Channel 23, which still was not part of Univision, but just the only Spanish channel operating in South Florida.

I also made radio and print media like The Miami Herald and Diario de las Américas and began to include my image as an essential part of the new car ads.

A new way of advertising rose with the popularization of entertainment programs on Hispanic TV, especially in Miami, where renowned TV figures were testing successful formulas to attract the attention of an audience hungry for new forms of entertainment.

It was there that I met many celebrities of local TV, among

them the late Rolando Barral, and a charismatic giant with a South American accent, who hardly anyone in Miami knew and started hosting a program from his native country, Chile.

Orange Bowl, TV and Carnival Parade

Like I said earlier, right after I started my new advertising strategy in Gus Machado Buick, opportunities began to pour.

The first of those came around mid 1982, a project by Gus Machado Buick and the Kiwanis of the Little Havana organization, to create and sponsor for the first time the famous Calle Ocho Festival.

The Kiwanis were at the time, and still are, a large organization (founded in 1916) dedicated to raise funds to help charitable causes of social impact related to children.

There were several Kiwanis chapters in South Florida, but it was the Little Havana club, founded seven years earlier, in 1975, that offered me to co-sponsor the event, in part I believe, because my budding popularity as a business figure resulting from the TV commercials.

The Little Havana event, eventually named *Paseo Carnaval*, was televised for the enjoyment of the entire community. The organizers unanimously decided that I should be the Master of Ceremonies of the televised event, and so it was.

By then, Miami had grown into an extra-large Cuban community, which had quadrupled its population after more

Gus Machado with Víctor Benítez and Tico Alonso, during the celebrations of the Ford Motor Credit Company's 10th anniversary, in 1994.

than 120,000 immigrants arrived in 1980 from the Port of Mariel, in Cuba, directly to Florida.

The advent of the *marielitos* took place within six months -April to October 1980-, all of them fleeing from the Castro dictatorship, by an agreement with the government of the president at the time, Jimmy Carter.

Truth is that the arrival of tens of thousands of compatriots was an event with multiple implications: creating new pressures for the local economy, which was flooded by the new labor force and new consumers with a different cultural baggage.

By 1982, many of these *marielitos* had managed to assimilate to their new country, generating on their end an economy which also required attention. That was one of the goals of the *Paseo Carnaval* project.

To initiate the great event, there was a caravan of floats parading along Flagler Street, departing from downtown Miami and reaching a stand on Southwest 8th Street, near the old Orange Bowl.

Thousands of people crowded the streets of Little Havana. My job was to keep that multitude excited with music, performances by popular guest artists. One time I had the opportunity to share the stage with Rocío Jurado, who helped me enliven the program.

Since the event was broadcast by Channel 23, the show had a great impact, boosting my car sales. Thanks to those events, our dealerships took first place here in Miami.

The success of *Paseo Carnaval* led me the next year to create a new event that would also become a great success.

It was a TV program for searching and promoting local artistic talent, to benefit young people who otherwise might not have an opportunity to succeed in life.

That was the type of activities with which I strongly identified. I have always been convinced that hard work and perseverance is the key to success, but for many working people there simply aren't enough opportunities to succeed in life.

There was another reason for which I liked the idea of

having an artistic and musical talent competition program. I always loved music and dance. Always enjoyed dance parties. So the idea of directing a music and dance program was simply the best of all.

The name of the program was our *Talentos*. At first we were broadcasting it using TV clips, and then it went live on Saturday nights.

Anyone who wanted to be on it could apply, and there were long lines at the Hialeah dealership, with a great many kids who were looking for a break.

Being the program's conductor, I was in a position to pick the jury, and all celebrities from the local radio were my friends.

The great stage for the program was the showroom where during the week the agencies' new cars were exhibited. Every Saturday we had to move all the cars out to a storage facility so that the set's decorations could be mounted.

We had several special guests on the program, the like of singers like Willy Chirino and Carlos Oliva.

We had competitions for the best dancers and the best vocal performers.

The program had a smashing success when two of the contestants who had won, Frank and Zobeida, were given the opportunity to represent the United States in the OTI Festival held in Seville, Spain, in 1985.

Not only did I discover Frank and Zobeida on my program *Nuestros Talentos*, but I also helped to produce their first

Gus in a yacht with friends filming one of the numerous commercials he produced to promote his business.

record, which included El canto de mi raza, the song they had interpreted at the OTI Festival.

The original purpose of the *Nuestros Talentos* was entertainment; however, it was bringing me good profits in business.

Thanks to the increase in sales, without thinking about it and trusting my good intuition, I decided in 1984 to get a new place for a second dealership that would be named Gus Machado Ford, which from the very beginning became the flagship for my business.

The following two years were of an intense activity to improve what I had really learned: not just selling cars, something about which I already knew enough to spare, but promotion and advertising, a new endeavor that thrilled me as I went along.

How I met Don Francisco

One day in 1986 I received in my office a visit from Mara Rankin, who was then the General Manager of Channel 23. She brought along with her a tallish gentleman with a distinct South American accent; and other executives from the channel, for the purpose of proposing a new project.

I was a advertising client in Channel 23, so I had a close professional relationship with the station General Manager, Joaquín Blaya, other executives like Omar Marchant, and the channel's star host, Rolando Barral.

The tallish South American was none other than the famous Chilean TV show host Mario Kreutzberger, better known as Don Francisco, who had just arrived to Miami and wanted to bring his show for the first time to our local television, and desperately needed a sponsor.

Don Francisco was already very famous in Chile, with his Saturday entertainment program that ran for as long as eight hours, and had tremendous ratings. He thought that bringing it to Miami for a Hispanic audience was a great idea.

It was a variety program with interviews, jokes, sketches and contests in which people could win money instantly by answering questions or could win larger prizes depending on

Gus used exotic locations to produce his trademark commercials, like this yacht in Biscayne Bay in June 1985.

the competition.

The truth is that after running four programs of *Sábado Gigante*, the show didn't take off nor grab a hold of the audience, and that's why they came to Gus Machado, in search of a willing sponsor for the program.

So I made a decision and on the fifth program, aired in August of 1986, the big prize offered for the contestants was a brand new yellow Buick, valued at $10,000, by courtesy of Gus Machado Buick of Hialeah. It was there and then that *Sábado Gigante* began to make history in Miami's television, with Gus Machado's sponsorship, which lasted about two years.

10

A new managerial style (1988-1991)

As I consolidated my business career thanks to the powerful tools of advertising and public relations, I also developed another parallel activity which had become, like music and dance, a personal passion.

As I said before, I owe my initiation into golf to my Puerto Rican friend Cándido González, who got me hooked on that sport in a very ingenious way, challenging me to hit the ball on the first swing.

I failed on my first try, but that failure led to practice. And the frequency with which I visited the driving range, which is where golfers practice the complicated swing, turned me into an addict of the sport, a fan of the tournaments and, of course, of the great golfers at the time.

I went deeper into the marvel of golf thanks to the numerous golf courses available, in some cases for decades, not only in

Miami but in Florida.

Proof of that, for example, are the old Miami Springs Golf Course, a venue famous for hosting the Miami Open from 1924 to 1955, and luminaries like Sam Snead, Fred Haas, Tommy Armour and Byron Nelson.

Another golf course with lineage was, and still is, the Doral's Blue Monster, opened in 1961 and venue of the legendary Doral Open from 1962 to 1969, and later on known as the Doral-Eastern Open (1970-1986), the Doral-Ryder Open (1987-2000), the Genuity Championship (2001-2002) and the Ford Championship at Doral (2003-2006), before being renamed the WGC-Cadillac Championship from 2007 to 2016.

Another golf course worthy of being mentioned is the historic Crandon Golf Club, located in Key Biscayne. Both the Crandon Golf Club and the Doral Blue Monster have a special significance for me, because it was there that I developed part of my phase as a sponsor of golf-related events, much to my satisfaction.

In 1985, when the event was called Doral-Eastern Open, I sponsored the first Golf Shoot Out Event, which is a brief competition preceding the main event, in which professional players participate, with prizes totaling $10,000, plus an additional $5,000 that I included for charitable causes of the American Cancer Association.

Ten noteworthy competitors participated: the legendary golfers Seve Ballesteros, Lee Trevino, Tom Kite, the Puerto

Gus Machado Ford's reopening ceremony after an extensive renovation in 2017. Left to right: Lydia Machado, Fausto and Remedios Díaz, the former Representative Ileana Ros-Lehtinen, Gus and Lilliam Machado, and Víctor Benítez.

Rican Chi Chi Rodríguez, Fred Couples, Andy Bean, Fuzzy Zoeller, Raymond Floyd and Denis Watson. At the end of the shootout two prevailed above the rest: Ballesteros and Couples.

At the end, I handed the biggest check to the great Seve Ballesteros: $2,500. Couples also received his part: $1,500 for his performance. Ballesteros won something additional: the right to drive for a whole year a latest model car, courtesy of Gus Machado Ford. I know that he enjoyed it, because Ballesteros at the time had a property in the Doral Resort complex, located at the Blue Monster, and he loved the lengthy seasons he spent in Miami.

That year's tournament was won by Mark McCumber,

followed in second place by Tom Kite, the previous year's winner. The winner took home $72,000, a great prize in those days.

The following year, I organized a similar event during the Doral Eastern Open 1986, won by Andy Bean for the third time, setting a record and winning for the effort a prize of $90,000.

After both events I was hooked by the prevailing atmosphere of the golfing competition, a combination of true camaraderie, high level competition and a charitable projection.

So, I went ahead and contacted the PGA Tour that handles all tournaments and golf events in the United States and elsewhere, to create a new tournament: the PGA Tour Senior Golf Classic in Miami, to be held at the Key Biscayne fabulous golf course.

So, in November 1987 the Gus Machado Senior Classic Golf Tournament at Key Biscayne was held, an event that brought together outstanding golf figures, national and local, in a high-ranking spirit and massive attendance.

Perhaps the event's most striking aspect was the prizes: a total of $300,000, a noteworthy figure provided by my companies. And additionally, but not less important: the entire event was going to be aired by the sports channel ESPN, meaning a tremendous impact from an advertising viewpoint for the brand Gus Machado Ford.

Thanks to some friends closely linked with the world of charity events, we managed to direct part of the tournament proceeds to the American Cancer Society and the United Way, two organizations I highly respected.

The tournament was won by the American golfer Gene Littler, better known as "Gene the Machine," who had won the US Open in 1961, and was known for his elegant swing to hit the ball.

In 1988 the tournament's second edition was held. Again, a large prize pool and ESPN's broadcast. The victory was for the Afro-American Lee Elder, who had the record of being the first one of his race to compete in the prestigious Master's Tournament.

My relationship with golf continued even though I was no longer a sponsor in the following years, to a large degree because other corporations with more financial muscle than ours, like the cruise company Royal Caribbean, which took over for the next 15 years as sponsor for the event I had founded in Crandon.

A decade later I decided to return to my earlier pursuits with the Gus Machado Classic Charity Golf Tournament, still going on more than 20 years later. But I'll get to that story later on.

A new partner arrives: Víctor Benítez

Near the end of the decade, in 1988, the business dynamics of Miami- Dade economy led me to make more radical decisions in search of new forms to make my business grow.

Gus Machado with a group of students from Westland Senior High School, during an event of the One Drive 4ur School program, created by Ford as a contribution to community education.

The United States economy had grown robustly thanks to the fiscally prudential policies, lower taxes and business stimulus, directed by President Ronald Reagan, who had been in the White House since 1981.

But Reagan's term was coming to a close. Aspiring to succeed him on the job, in seeking a third Republican term was his Vice President, George H. W. Bush, in a formula with Senator Dan Quayle for the November elections that year.

By the way, years later I met President Bush Sr., but that's a personal anecdote and I'll get to it later.

After Pope John Paul II's visit to Miami in November 1987,

the new year, 1988, had started with a great bustle in sports, and I was keenly observing the details, because sports and car sales go hand in hand, as I had confirmed with golf.

The University of Miami's football team, the Hurricanes won a crushing victory that had nationwide resonance against Oklahoma's team in a memorable game at the bygone Orange Bowl of Miami.

Miami was in the process of growing, after the first generation of Cuban exiles began to make their presence felt. I looked for ways to adapt my managerial structure and after some changes in personnel, I decided to bring along a young and very dynamic manager to be my right hand for advancing in this new stage.

My intuition was provenly confirmed when after several months of testing, the manager, Víctor Benítez, early in 1988 became not only the second aboard my business organization, but a full-fledged partner.

I had met Víctor through a mutual friend, Gregorio Santiesteban, who was in the used car business and had a car lot near our business. I had a great friendship with Gregorio because both of us had been in the auto trade for years.

One day I commented to Gregorio that I was looking for a new manager for our Ford dealership in Hialeah, and asked him to let me know if he knew a good candidate.

That was when Víctor came into the picture. He was not a newcomer but an experienced manager who had been working

Gus Machado supported numerous charity projects, among them the Miami Children's Hospital Foundation.

for eight years with other entrepreneurs in the same trade, the well-known Potamkin Group, and was looking for new opportunities on the market.

But Víctor had his own plans. He didn't want to be just an employee, but wanted to be part of my business as a shareholding partner.

He told me that that was how he had worked in the past and that it was a layout in which he would feel comfortable.

"I come from a working relationship where I was part owner, the only way I would be interested in working with you is by being part of the business," he told me in a very frank manner.

"*Chico*, if that is the way in which you have worked before, and evidently you have been successful, I am ready to try it," I told Víctor, well aware that in business relationships, partners also assume the risks and do everything possible to achieve success because they are also working for their own interests.

Before closing the deal in writing, with lawyers and notaries, we agreed that a six-month trial period would be judicious. So that's how it was. Around mid 1988, Víctor and I signed an agreement of share participation in which I would be the senior partner and Víctor would hold a lesser portion of shares.

The day we signed the agreement marked the beginning of a relationship that has lasted, to this day, with ups and downs, more than 30 years. The sturdiness of that business relationship was tested sooner than what Víctor and I expected.

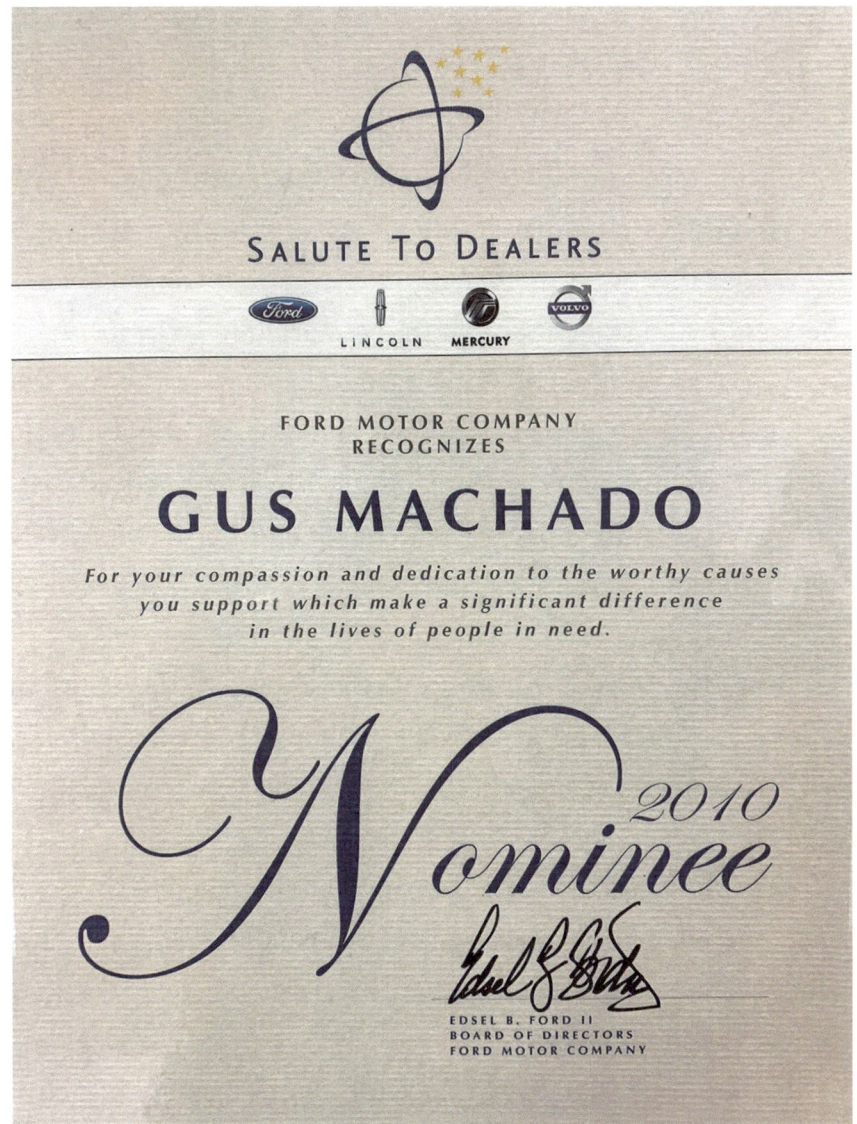

For years the Ford Corporation recognized Gus Machado's success and the noble causes sponsored by him, his family and the automobile business, which made a difference on the life of needy persons, as shown by this 2010 recognition.

A great team to push forward the Gus Machado brand

The Ford agency in Hialeah, unlike the other Buick agency, was going through a spat of difficulties for reasons that are not relevant at this point the person in charge of management left the agency, and right after that things started to go awry.

At a later moment Víctor told me that one of the reasons for his decision to come to work with me was my popularity on local TV. My constant appearances on the screen, advertising with a broad smile our products, Buick and Ford, definitively were a great boost for sales, and as far as that was concerned he wasn't off-target.

From the very beginning Víctor assumed the roles of general manager and group vice president, and his job was practically supervising all the departments to ensure they were running correctly.

Víctor joined a work team that included the well-remembered George Koennig, and a year later Ana Arisso was added, someone who has been my loyal and efficient secretary for more than 30 years.

At the time our Gus Machado Ford agency had five departments: the new and used cars department; the service department, the parts and repair (bodyshop) department, and finally the accounting department, which was like a central nervous system, where all the operations has to go through.

Gus Machado and Víctor Benítez with a customer during an event of the One Drive 4 Ur School program, conceived by Ford Motor Company to serve the community.

Each department had its own manager and a junior manager reporting to the vice president and then directly to me.

We had established the discipline of meeting every day to discuss the operations and evaluate each detail of how we could improve business. It was an evaluation of day-to-day activities to which I paid much attention, although Víctor was in charge of all daily operations.

The professional way in which Víctor began to run the departments earned my trust to the point that I could devote myself to the part of business I liked most: advertising and public relations.

Although at the time I was basically in charge of all the advertising strategy, Víctor joined me immediately, suggesting ideas not just to boost sales at the Ford agency, but at the Buick agency as well.

Víctor joined the advertising strategy mostly because he came from an automobile group that was highly regarded when it came to advertising, and that was just what we needed.

Back then, as it is now, I think that we made a great team: I, Gus Machado, image and face of the business; Víctor, taking care of the operational details behind the scenes, next to George and Ana.

That year things were organized at the agency and we recovered the sales flow level that we were used to.

The following year, 1989, was a good year also. The Republicans had won the November elections in 1988 for the third time, this time by George W. H. Bush, and Reagan's fiscal policy continued practically uninterrupted.

That year had started with a mixture of euphoria and violence. On one side, the local football team, the Miami Hurricanes, won a roaring victory at the Orange Bowl for the third time. But racially motivated riots were unleashed as the result of a shooting in Overtown, extending to Liberty City, two enclaves of the local Afro-American population.

Thank God, the lootings following the confrontation did not affect our agencies.

A more difficult stage developed unexpectedly towards the end of the decade, extending to the beginning of the next one, as a result of several events whose causes were way beyond our control.

Surviving a hurricane and an international war

In 1989, Gus Machado's emporium included the Ford and Buick agencies in Hialeah, which produced the bulk of our annual revenue, and a car rental operation in Puerto Rico as a Budget franchise.

But two factors completely modified that corporate structure that had generated so many benefits.

The first of those factors was a climate phenomenon causing severe damages in Puerto Rico and other Caribbean islands, hurricane Hugo, a storm that reached the maximum destruction capacity (Category 5, on the Saffir-Simpson Scale) that a phenomenon of this kind can reach.

The hurricane formed on September 10 and a week later struck the island, with the unusual ferocity of winds lashing in excess of 160 miles per hour, causing extensive blackouts and leaving about 28,000 people homeless, and 8 fatalities as a result of the storm.

The destruction of the island's infrastructure was heavy. According to official estimates, Hugo caused losses approaching a billion dollars in damages to property and crops.

Hugo's hurricane force winds did not reach Miami (they went as far north as the coast of South Carolina, before dissipating on September 25th), but damages and losses were felt in our offices, casting concern about the status of our assets.

According to the inventories, our Budget car rental business had a flotilla of 1,200 automobiles. But the problem was not the status of that inventory, which was safe and did not suffer any major damages. The fundamental worry was the immediate economic future of an island shaken to its foundation by a category 5 hurricane.

Indeed, as we had foreseen, the disaster caused by the storm diminished economic activity on the island, particularly tourism, practically to zero. The following months of 1989 and the first ones of 1990 were depressive for business.

By then not even 50 tourists a week visited Puerto Rico, thus impacting severely our operations on the island.

Gus Machado and his wife Lilliam were great donors of the American Cancer Society for many years.

It was necessary to make a decision: sell the business to the best bidder to cover the losses and the still pending debts. Thank God, all the debts were covered, every single dollar owed.

I took the step after much thinking and with great sorrow because I had been doing business in Puerto Rico since the late '60s and I had done quite well, besides cultivating important and lasting friendships. But in business, losses are a no-no and it made no sense to hang on to that business venture that had been badly stricken by the winds remaining in the post-hurricane season.

Now, while concentrating on the two operations, Ford and Buick, It didn't take long for us to be impacted by a new event that no one could have foreseen in the least bit.

Early in August 1990, a war conflict miles away in the Middle East, had an impact that was strongly felt everywhere, with consequences affecting many businesses, including ours in Hialeah.

It was the invasion of Kuwait ordered by the Iraqi dictator, Saddam Hussein. On that August thousands of Iraqi soldiers invaded Kuwaiti territories, a country holding one of the world's largest oil reserves.

For whatever reason it was, Hussein's initiative unleashed a powerful international reaction: a coalition of 34 countries headed by the United States was organized to fight a war that began on January 1991, with the awe-inspiring bombings by naval and air forces against Iraqi positions in Baghdad, the capital, and areas of Kuwait occupied by Hussein's troops.

It was truly a light show for the entire world to see, thanks to CNN's live broadcast, something never seen before.

After the Puerto Rican fiasco, sales were recovering their pace. To give you an idea, on December 1990, a month before the bombings we had managed to sell 380 units in Hialeah's

Gus Machado during an automotive industry event in Detroit, Michigan.

Ford agency, a very respectable figure for a Miami dealer.

But when the United States and its allies went to war, practically all the attention and many resources shifted to the war conflict, affecting the local economy, including car dealerships.

From the 380 units sold in December 1990, we dropped to barely 90 units in January of 1991, when the air and naval bombings started and extended for the rest of that month.

It seemed as if the world had stopped, no one really knew if the end of the world was around the corner, because the dictator Hussein had promised "the mother of all battles," including possible attacks on American soil.

None of that happened, but at the moment that worry was lashing at everybody's mind all over the world, especially because it had been a long time since the United States had been involved in an international war like the Gulf War, as the conflict came to be known.

The war formally ended late in February 1991 with the occupation of Iraq. But the economic consequences were devastating for many businesses in Miami.

Many banks such as CenTrust and South East, forced by the bad economy, closed its Miami branches. Other companies, like Spanish Broadcasting Systems (SBS), that controlled important Spanish language radio stations, went bankrupt.

The reason behind those bankruptcies was that many of those businesses had loans from financial institutions that, for reasons not worth mentioning, had been seized by the government. And due to the war requirements, those institutions had demanded payments of those loans at a moment in which many businesses didn't have the available cash.

So, many of those indebted businesses decided to seek protection under bankruptcy laws. Had it not been for that emergency situation those difficulties would have been easily overcome. But this was not our case.

Our situation was complicated. We had two mortgages with AmeriFirst, and since we had skipped payments for a few months due to business difficulties, the mortgages were foreclosed.

AmeriFirst was one of those firms seized by the government, and was demanding payments. Unless there was a viable solution, the bank was ready to seize my two companies, just like that.

The situation was so difficult that we were forced to make another radical decision: selling the Buick dealership, which owned the land it was on. With that sale, to the Home Depot chain, we covered the outstanding debt with GMC, Buick's financier, and closed the agency.

To cover the $5 million owed by Gus Machado Ford to AmeriFirst, which had already filed a claim in a Miami court, I had the luck and ability to get a $4.6 million loan from Ford Motor Credit Corp., to avoid foreclosure, or close the Ford agency.

Had it not been for that vital loan from Ford, I don't know what would have happened.

At the journey's end, in August 1991, we were able to get out of that mess unscathed, although depleted, but kept Gus Machado Ford in business.

As Víctor used to state crystally clear: "We never went bankrupt, we never cheated anyone. Gus Machado fulfilled all his obligations and paid everyone to the last penny."

On that occasion I stated to The Miami Herald that the payment agreement "will keep me in business and, I hope, for the rest of my life." I wasn't wrong when I made that prediction.

11

Corporate challenges (1992-2001)

What a hurricane and an international war inflicted on our business organization, severely hurting our finances and pushing us to the edge of a precipice, another disaster, paradoxically brought life to it, and its consequences would last for several years.

Until the early '90s we had to navigate the vicissitudes of a powerful storm wiping out our car rental business in Puerto Rico. And when we least expected a war conflict broke out in the Persian Gulf leaving us and many other Miami entrepreneurs on the brink of bankruptcy.

Businesses that had prospered for decades found themselves forced to close down, overwhelmed by debts which had to be paid all of a sudden. Many of them lacked the financial capability to honor those debts and were left with no choice other than going out of business.

In our case the blow was so severe that besides the loan I secured from Ford, I was even forced to mortgage a property I had acquired in the exclusive Indian Creek Country Club, a private community on Miami Beach, where I had prominent neighbors like Don Francisco, Julio Iglesias, and my dear friends Don Shula and his wife Mary Ann.

A bit more than a year after the fateful Gulf War, Miami became the scenario of a new catastrophic event, which rattled the foundations of wide areas in South Florida, like it had not happened in many decades.

The event, like all tragedies, took us all by surprise because there was no way to predict neither the meteorological phenomenon nor its impact. But neither was there a way of foreseeing the effect it would have on our corporate operations.

A new hurricane revives business

Hurricane Andrew struck with catastrophic winds on August 24, 1992, first in Elliot Key and later south of Miami, with intense category 5 winds. The passing of the gigantic hurricane lasted a few hours, but the devastation it left in his path was monumental and unprecedented.

In Hialeah the storm was felt with less intensity because the hurricane's eye passed further south, at the heart of the city of Homestead, but the deluge that came down caused damages all around.

Gus Machado with James Murphy, organizer of "12 Good Men", an event sponsored by the Ronald McDonald House Charities, to recognize South Florida business leaders for their charity work.

The violent gusts and the ensuing floods affected whole neighborhoods throughout Miami-Dade County. The damages were more extensive that those caused by hurricane Hugo in Puerto Rico.

But unlike Hugo, hurricane Andrew's desolation affected not only thousands of homes, left roofless or with serious structural damages, but also causing the loss of thousands of vehicles all over the county, many of them literally covered with water up to the roof.

In a city like Miami, with limited access to public transportation, and a restricted Metro service, a vehicle isn't

Gus and Lilliam Machado were selected in 2013 as part of a group of 12 leaders recognized for their dedication to community causes, by the Ronald McDonald House Charities.

just an indispensable tool for work but also for moving around for health or entertainment needs.

Therefore, during the days that followed hurricane Andrew, we began to receive reports of hundreds of vehicles damaged by the storm.

It wasn't only the vehicles. Andrew left significant human and structural losses in all of Florida, adding up to 44 lives and the incredible figure of $25 billion in economic damages.

The hurricane also brought many changes to Miami-Dade, mainly in building codes and also to the security of power lines, the supply chains for emergency help and evacuation plans.

No one was ready for what came later. We didn't have the slightest idea of what kind of vehicle demand was going to erupt a few weeks after the hurricane.

The sales figures jumped to an unprecedented level.

On September 1992, barely a month after Andrew, Gus Machado Ford sold 560 units, when normally we sold an average of 350.

Everything was selling: sedans, trucks, low consumption vehicles as well as gas guzzlers.

As of that moment we began to rise and rise, and the sales upshoot did not stop climbing during the final months of that year, continuing to be unstoppable for all of 1993 and 1994.

In consideration to the families that suffered heavy economic losses, we created programs to facilitate financing, so that those people could have a chance to replace vehicles lost during the storm.

Little by little we began to climb to the level of the dealers with the highest sales volume in the region, and then, as expected, we faced new corporate challenges before us.

For the period from 1992 to 1995, we became one of the top Ford dealers in all the United States, a great distinction when you consider that there were more than 4,300 dealers in the entire nation.

Two big and powerful allies

By that time the Gus Machado brand was soundly established. The public events I attended had placed me on a prestigious position in the community. I've never liked to show off, but I can't deny that I am a very sociable person, with many relationships, and that was a part of my job that I really loved doing.

I remember what my secretary for many years, Ana Arisso, used to tell me. She was very young, in the late '80s, when she started working in my office, and she remembered what her grandmother said when she heard that Ana had been hired by Gus Machado Ford.

"Oh, it's excellent that you're going to work with the artist Gus Machado! He is on all the TV programs and he's very famous."

Ana, by the way, was the person who kept tab of my complicated agenda, which could include in any given day visits from Ford executives, local leaders and television personalities or managers; or meetings about how to improve relations with customers, sellers and employees, until late into the night.

Among the personalities with whom I established a solid relationship was the well-remembered and renowned editor Alvah Chapman, who presided the newspaper chain Knight-Ridder for decades and was the CEO of The Miami Herald since the '60s.

During the Ronald McDonald House Charities' 12 Good Men Awards, in March 2013. Gus is accompanied by Víctor Benítez, Gus Machado Ford's Manager, Ana Arisso, Lydia Machado, Myra Dewhurst and Lilliam Machado's daughter, Gigi.

We met in many of the events in which we coincided. Later we became close friends because we shared the same passion for golf, which he practiced as frequently as his health allowed.

I can say that I learned a lot from Alvah, like no other businessman or anyone else from the media.

He was a man who came from a family of newspaper editors from Columbus, Georgia, and served for almost 30 years as chairman of the editorial group Knight Ridder, whose flagship newspaper was The Miami Herald.

I met him precisely when he was a frequent figure at Miami's more important corporate and social events.

For me one of Chapman's most admirable facets was his philanthropic dedication. He played a crucial role in helping to rebuild parts of Miami- Dade County's south that were the worst hit by hurricane Andrew, and he sponsored all kinds of cultural and citizen's efforts.

He presided the Florida Philharmonic Orchestra as his principal promoter; was a member of the Miami Coalition for a Drug-Free Community, the Goodwill Industries of South Florida, the Greater Miami Chamber of Commerce, and Miami Citizens against Crime, among others.

He created Chapman Partnership, the Miami organization dedicated, like no other, to helping the homeless for 25 years, and on several occasions we attended it's annual galas.

In 2001, he helped establish an important grant for the Alvah H. Chapman Jr. Business School at Florida International University, an idea that I borrowed a decade and a half later.

As with many other people with whom I was close friends, I shared many 18 holes games with Alvah, who was an avid golfer like me.

Besides golf, we coincided in our liking for stories inspired by the word of God.

One time, Alvah gave me as a present a copy of a little book that he received as part of a monthly subscription, with stories based on biblical messages. The little book was actually a spiritual devotional titled The Upper Room. Immediately I ordered several subscriptions, not only for my kids but also for my closest employees at Gus Machado Ford. I kept the subscription for many years, and it served me as a source of inspiration in difficult times, thanks to Alvah.

Another personality who chose to call his new home Miami, like I did, and who also experienced great success here, was my well-remembered and dear friend Don Shula.

The great football coach, a historical figure in that sport, left in his wake a strong imprint on our South Florida community.

Not only was he the first coach to lead his team in six Super Bowls, five of them with the Miami Dolphins; he has been the only one to complete a perfect season in the history of the NFL, in 1972, when he won his first Super Bowl.

Don's list of accomplishments in sports are endless. I just want to emphasize my admiration for his career, which I especially followed closely during the time we were neighbors in Indian Creek, where he and his wonderful wife, Mary Anne, shared with us countless charity and social events, and during which Don displayed his flair as an influential personality.

Much like Alvah and I, Don was also particularly interested as much in golf as in the Christian faith.

In his youth he wanted to become a catholic priest, but gave it up when he realized that the priesthood would not allow him to develop his other passion, football, first as a player and later as a top-notch coach.

Don Shula developed a personal style for business after he retired from coaching, a legacy that has remained active thanks

Gus Machado presents the 2015 Gus Machado Golf Classic Humanitarian Award to his friend Don Shula. Also on the stage: Mary Ann Shula and Lillian Machado.

to the efforts of his sons. And he certainly was no stranger to charitable causes, donating money and time for cancer research.

Alvah and Don are examples of community leadership that have influenced my own career as a businessman, an influential personality and promoter of charitable causes.

How I met three presidents of the United States

The resurgence of Gus Machado Ford, after the streak of

financial difficulties, brought good news. Our success in sales brought along nationwide recognition.

The first of the recognitions came in late 1992, when we were Number One in South Florida. The award had encores in 1993, 1994, 1995 and 1996, the last one being the apex of our success in the trade.

In 1994 and 1995 we were included on the list of the 100 Ford dealerships with the highest number of sales, an outstanding recognition considering that there were more than 4,200 dealers nationwide.

The recognition was not just a plaque with the name Gus Machado Ford on it, but also a trip with all expenses paid to an automobile salesmen convention.

In 1995 the convention was held in San Diego, California. Present there was a group 100 top sellers of Ford vehicles, a group to which belonging was a privilege.

The convention was an occasion to share, network and enjoy a well- deserved rest over a long weekend. Also included, for my delight, was a round of golf on a splendid golf course, one of many existing in the city.

It was in that scenario that I had the good fortune to meet another great personality, the event's special guest, who also happened to have a weakness for golf.

On Friday morning I was in the locker room getting ready to begin the day on the green along the rest of my colleagues, also aficionados to golf, when I had the surprise of seeing a very well-

Gus Machado was a pioneer in the use of mass communication technologies to promote his businesses.

known figure: the former president, George W. H. Bush. "It can't be anyone else," I thought, so I ventured to approach him.

I felt at ease because I knew personally one of the president's sons, Jeb, who a year before had been a candidate for governor in Florida. Although he didn't win, in Miami's Cuban community we backed him up all the way.

"Mr. President," I said without any preambles. "I'm a good friend of your son Jeb. I'm Gus Machado, of Gus Machado Ford in Hialeah."

I wasn't expecting him to know who I was, but just the same, I let him know who I was, and placed myself at his service if he came to visit us in Florida.

President Bush, with his typical charisma, greeted me warmly and for the following five minutes, we had a most pleasant chat. From there we went outdoors to start the round. I was very pleased of having shared a moment with a historical figure of his caliber.

The following day, all the guests met in a great hall for the gala dinner in which the keynote speaker was President Bush.

After a great exposition, came the questions and answers session, as usual in this sort of event.

The first questions had to do with the economy, the effects of the Democrat policies of Bill Clinton, among other subjects.

It was then that I decided to request the microphone to formulate, from the back of the hall, my question:

"Mr President, what do you think it's going to happen in Cuba when Fidel Castro dies?"

President Bush paused pensively for a few seconds, trying to spot the person who asked the question.

"I know that Latino accent," he said. "Is that you, Gus?"

Many in the audience who knew me, started laughing. Others were surprised that in just two days, I was someone known to the former President Bush.

"*Coño*, Gus," said a colleague who knew me from other events. "I didn't know that you knew President Bush."

Gus Machado was also a pioneer in bringing over professional golfers and football players in his marketing campaigns to promote his car dealership.

George H. W. Bush was not the only president I met personally. I had the good fortune to meet other great American presidents after they retired.

I met the great leader Ronald Reagan during an event in which I had the chance to shake his hand. Reagan is perhaps one of the American presidents I most admire, for his role in the downfall of international communism.

I also had the good fortune to meet and shake hands with another great president, Gerald Ford, who succeeded Richard Nixon after his untimely exit, and had governed the United States amidst great difficulties.

Gus and Lilliam Machado during a Miami Dolphins baseball game.

Gus Machado's social sensitivity

From the time of my arrival to Hialeah in 1956, when I properly began my career as an entrepreneur, I fought with all my might to attain success, grow, expand and consolidate in the business I had learned, which I liked, and gave me satisfaction and opportunities.

Parallel to my quest for success in business, to which I dedicated countless work hours, surged another need that became imperative: the need to give, to contribute, to offer opportunities to the less fortunate.

It was the moment new initiatives like *Nuestros Talentos* arose, to promote youngsters who didn't have an opportunity to break into the competitive artistic world.

Then came the Golf Championship for senior golfers in Key Biscayne, `to help the programs of the American Cancer Society.

We constantly had programs for the donation of school supplies to help low-income residents of Hialeah.

More ambitious initiatives would come later on.

With the intention to unite my penchant for helping with my passion for golf and the contacts I had made at that point, in 1998 I founded the Gus Machado Classic Charity Tournament, for the benefit of the Cancer Society.

It wasn't only for the enjoyment of a healthy day playing golf and meeting friends, but also a great effort to collect funds. The event's success, still ongoing in 2021, has been as resonant as my efforts to sell automobiles during more than six decades.

My efforts in this world brought me, by chance or by the art of magic, new acquaintances that enriched my life like never before. One of these acquaintances, the most special, opened for me a new an unexpected world that made me understand more fully the true meaning of life.

At the center of that universe: a very special woman who, without intending it, changed my life for the better.

12

My life with Lilliam (2001)

My relationship with Lilliam started in a fortuitous manner. I was attending a convention in Texas in the early '20s, where I was participating as member of the *Cámara de Comercio Latina* (Camacol), to which I had belonged for many years.

It was the era in which George W. Bush still was the governor of Texas.

I was there with a delegation presided by my friend William Alexander, whom I knew since the '70s. He had participated in the Bay of Pigs invasion in Cuba and had been one of the pioneer pilots on the first flights of Eastern Airlines between Miami and Latin America, before becoming an entrepreneur and distinguished unionist.

I had been single for some time, two years to be exact, and had no commitments after two long marriages that ended in separation.

Also at that Texan convention were my dear friends Fausto and Remedios Díaz Oliver, who greeted me warmly when we ran into each other in the hotel's lobby.

"Gus, what a pleasure to see you, how have you been?" Remedios asked me.

I told the truth about what was happening in my life.

"I'm doing well, divorced two years ago, but I'm now taking care of my businesses."

I didn't know it then, but later found out that after that conversation, both of them thought that I had been alone for too long and it wasn't doing me any good, so they took the initiative, on their own, to find me a mate for life.

Unbeknownst to me, right after we returned to Miami, Remedios concurred with William Alexander and both of them arranged a blind date with someone, who they thought was going to understand me marvelously.

"It's someone you'll love," Remedios told me one day. "We already arranged the blind date. The party is on Saturday. We expect you without fail," she made me promise to go.

"Whatever you say, Remedios," I said without paying much attention, and practically forgot all about it.

When the day arrived, I went to the party a bit baffled, but without much stress, because I was ready to enjoy the evening, have a few drinks, dance and have a good time, without really thinking much about the prospective date.

Gus and Lilliam Machado on their wedding night in Las Vegas, April 26, 2011.

I arrived at the party and sat at a table to wait for my friends. Fausto showed up and approached me right away.

"Hey, Machado, you here already? Are you by yourself?"

"Hi Fausto, here I am, supposedly for a blind date but I haven' seen her yet."

It was obvious that Fausto wasn't aware of what Remedios and William had planned.

"And what's the name of that person you're about to meet tonight," asked Fausto.

"It's a lady they are going to introduce me to, her name is Lilliam Martínez."

"Lilliam Martínez?" said Fausto, surprised. On the spot he took me by the arm and said:

"Come, let's have a drink." He took me to the bar, poured me a glass of Scotch, and placing an arm over my shoulder, he opened up:

"Gus Machado, I know you, but there's nothing in the world that would please me more than to see you marrying Lilliam Martínez."

Without any delay, I reacted:

"I don't know that girl and you're already marrying me to her!" I told Fausto.

Fausto smiled, took me once again by the arm and led me to the table where he was sitting with Remedios and other guests. The girl I was about to meet that night was right there, the famous Lilliam.

Gus and Lilliam represented for many years one of the most influential couples in South Florida's philanthropy and business scene.

"Gus, let me introduce my dear friend Lilliam," said Remedios, with a gesture of satisfaction and an impish smile on her face.

"Pleased to meet you," I said to Lilliam with a smile, extending my hand over the table.

Fausto blurted: "And you, Remedios, we came together in the car with Lilliam and you said nothing about this blind date."

All of us laughed.

Shortly later I realized that Remedios intuition wasn't off track, because Lilliam and I stayed together for the rest of the party. We chatted about everything and danced all night. To me it seemed as if I had been dancing with her all my life.

I liked a lot the mutual understanding, the connaturality with which we treated each other, and not feeling any kind of pressure, especially because I was in no hurry to get involved with anyone.

It was clear that both of us had recently divorced from our respective former partners. And each one of us had a family, businesses, and life. And that's what I liked about it.

Later I learned that Lilliam knew who I was, of course, on account of my presence on TV; but she was surprised because she had expected to find a different man from the one she found.

"You're not the Gus I had in my mind," Lilliam revealed afterwards. Not only did I strike her as a very pleasant person, for her very demanding taste; but she was surprised by how well I danced and how much I liked to sing, because she liked exactly the same two things.

The *perils* of love

When the party ended I knew that the *peril* of romance had started. She said to me:

"How good to find someone who likes dancing as much as I do."

Lilliam and Gus Machado with their great friend Don Shula, the legendary NFL player, coach and Hall of Fame member.

But, frankly, the day after the party I went back to my bachelor's working routine, and I didn't think anymore about the blind date. All of that smelled of falling in love and, therefore, *danger*.

Two weeks later, William Alexander invited me to a new Camacol event, this time an informal cocktail to meet new members of the chamber. When I arrived, the place was very crowded, and I found an unexpected scene.

Next to the podium, on a stand, was someone playing a guitar. And microphone in hand was my dear Lilliam, singing boleros with a voice that jolted me.

When she finished singing, I approached her with a greeting. After the cocktail I invited her to dinner, and from there we went dancing. Lilliam was charming and friendly with me. It was another extraordinary evening.

On the following weekend we went out again, and then facing me she told me, quite frankly, how she felt:

"Come here, how come you didn't call me after the time we met in a blind date, not even to thank me? Because I know that you had a good time with me."

With a smile, I replied on the spot:

"Because I know that this smells of danger." "What smells of danger?" she countered.

"Having met, having a good time, how we danced, that smells of danger. I wasn't into complicating myself now, but well…" I said leaving a question in the air.

Gus and Lilliam Machado were for decades one of the most outstanding South Florida couples for their participation on charitable causes.

The result of that outing was that from then on, we began to go out regularly every week.

The dates were with mutual friends, and almost always we ended dancing all night. That seemed like a marathon. On those evenings one of our favorite places was the now closed Diego's Restaurant, in Coral Gables, which combined a magnificent menu of Spanish dishes with good Cuban music.

Other days we went out to dinner and then ended in some of those quaint Little Havana spots, listening to Cuban jam sessions. We used to dance as if we had been doing it all our lives, something that impressed me, but also worried me.

Although I was trying to keep the relationship at a moderate pace, inevitably we began to see each other more frequently. I would pick her up at her house, where she lived with her mother, and almost immediately that lady grew fond of me.

It couldn't be any other way: hers was a hardworking and honest family that had come from Cuba, fleeing from communism. A story worth telling.

Lilliam's trajectory

Lilliam's family came from a small town named Amarillas, I know not why, in the Matanzas province. Since her father, Don Osmundo Sánchez, worked at the Por Fuerza Sugar Mill, belonging to the Arrechabala family of Cárdenas. She practically grew up there.

When she was 15, her parents, especially thanks to her mother, Doña Violeta de Sánchez, sent her to Matanzas to study for becoming a kindergarten teacher, which was what she liked most and was within her reach. There she spent two years studying at a private school for girls that aspired to be teachers.

Her parents placed her in a nun's boarding house while she attended a non-religious private school, because her parents felt more confident about her staying there.

That period started in 1958 and lasted until 1959, when the school was closed by orders from Fidel Castro. When the regime told the students that they would have to continue their schooling in coed state schools, Lilliam decided to drop out.

Her father, who was still working at the sugar mill, brought her back home and had her return to her previous piano studies, as before she had been sent to the private school.

"Come back here and stick to studying piano and your things because this will pass and then you can return to school," said her father without imagining what was to come.

At the age of 17, in January 1960, she married for the first time and started her own first family. She got pregnant and while she was recovering in a clinic after giving birth to a beautiful girl, early in October of that year, the unimaginable happened.

Fidel Castro ordered the first of a policy of massive confiscations of commercial and private properties, all of which passed to the hands of the State without any kind of compensation to their original owners.

The enactment of that policy created such panic that many families decided on the spot to leave Cuba and come to the United States. That was how, with her 17-day-old daughter, along with her husband and his family, Lilliam left Cuba on October 23, 1960, never to return.

Her parents, just like mine, came later to Miami escaping from the Castroite disaster.

For the next three decades, Lilliam dedicated herself basically to raise her family. She had three children, and these gave her grandchildren. She never had to work before her divorce in the late '90s.

Her first job was, after some training, as manager of the Hamilton Bank in Miami.

While at the bank, she received a business proposal from her friend Remedios, to join in a partnership for distributing canned foods of the Spanish brand Molinera in the United States.

The products were pimentos and other preserves that were number one in the market. Also canned fruits, vegetables and other products of Spanish cuisine.

For her it was an adventure because she had never been in charge of her own business. But capabilities she had to spare and the Molinera distribution business was a great success.

An unforeseen marriage

From the moment we met, early in the 2000s, we had a

Gus and Lilliam Machado focused on programs to benefit communities in South Florida, throughout their extensive philanthropic activity.

relationship marked by the enjoyment of the good life and respect for each other's lives.

Certainly, I was in no hurry to formalize our relationship, and neither did she. As incredible as it may seem, we kept our relationship in those conditions for a decade.

Frequently, I dined at her place, and she accompanied me

in my Miami Beach bachelor's apartment. Occasionally we got together to share a good meal or a Sunday dinner with her children.

We frequented mutual friends, shared parties and celebrations, and even travelled to our favorite destinations taking advantage of the Ford conventions to which I was invited every year. But we went each on one's own, until the day when everything changed unexpectedly.

In one of our trips, we went to Las Vegas to attend one of the Ford conventions. Lilliam told her friend Remedios about the trip because she knew that for her Las Vegas was an irresistible place.

Remedios was in Denver, Colorado, attending a meeting of the board of directors of the US West telephone company, of which she was a member, and she didn't think twice about it:

"We're on our way there," replied Remedios on the phone.

On that occasion we travelled with Víctor Benítez and his wife Idania, nicknamed Dana, in representation of Gus Machado Ford at the convention.

The night we got there the three couples we went out to dine at an exclusive Vegas restaurant, and when we came back to the hotel, I made a comment to Lilliam, whose birthday was coming up.

"Look, I want to give you a surprise for your birthday," I said without further ado.

Puzzled, she stared me in the eyes.

Gus and Lilliam Machado surrounded by children and grandchildren of the Machado family in Miami.

Of course, she could not imagine what I had in mind. For truth's sake, neither did I. It simply occurred to me that day, like something that couldn't wait any longer.

"What do you say we get married here? Why not take advantage of being here in Vegas and get married?"

"Here... in Vegas?" asked Lilliam somewhat unimpressed. "Well, they say it's easier here. Why not take advantage of that?"

"Are you crazy? How on earth am I going to get married without my kids and my grandchildren? No way!" she replied.

"Let's say we get married and later, when we are back in

Miami, you throw the party you want," I countered.

"No, I can't do that to my kids and grandchildren, no way!" Lilliam was hell-bent on the subject.

"If I'm going to marry you, it has to be in front of my kids and grandchildren," she added.

I did not insist and simply turned around and forgot the issue.

Apparently, Lilliam consulted her pillow that night and then with Remedios, because the next day, early in the morning, she told me that she wanted to reconsider my proposal.

"With respect to what you said last night, my answer now is: yes, I do!" she said without further preambles.

"Well, in that case, let's go right now and make the arrangements," I said. I rented a limousine to drive us around to whichever of the many chapels that are open for 24 hours a day would be the correct one.

After seeing a few of them, Lilliam said: "Let's get married in a more private place."

So that's what we did. We reserved a private hall in an exclusive restaurant inside the Bellagio Hotel, whose owner was a Spanish entrepreneur that had been highly recommended to us. We spoke to the owner and all the necessary reservations were arranged.

Our good friends Remedios and Fausto, who had been staying at the Bellagio, took charge of finding the pastor for the private ceremony.

Gus and Lilliam Machado with members of the Martinez-Sanchez branch of the family in Miami.

On the wedding day, April 26, 2011, I went to play golf with the friends at the Ford convention. That day was the peak of the convention: Ford was going to unveil the new models ready for launching on the market.

After ending the golf round, we had lunch and got ready for the plenary session, scheduled for 5:30 p.m. With all the day's hustle, and greetings colleagues, it seemed as if the moment for the private ceremony would never arrive.

Lilliam whispered to me:

"We have to go."

But I kept greeting friends.

"It's getting late," insisted Lilliam. "Remedios has already given three glasses of wine to the reverend," she insisted.

I said, still distracted: "Now we're leaving." Until Lilliam squeezed my arm and said:

"Gus, it's time, we have to go get married." At last, I gave in, and we left at full speed.

When we reached the restaurant, Remedios and Fausto were there, Víctor and Dana, next to the justice of the peace. On a table there was a bouquet of Lilliam's favorite flowers.

At the moment in which the vows were supposed to be pronounced, the pastor asked aloud:

"And the rings?"

Suddenly I realized that with all the commotion, we had forgotten that detail.

But, not wasting any time, Víctor stepped forward saying: "Here they are," offering his own rings and his wife Dana's.

All of us smiled after Víctor's quick solution, we took the borrowed rings, and the wedding proceeded.

After the simple ceremony, Lilliam called her sons to let them know.

The only thing that Lilliam lamented was that her mother was no longer around to give her the good news.

Upon returning to Miami, Lilliam threw her party full blast. And then we went on a trip to Europe, and I made good use of it by including my annual visit to Scotland to play golf with a select group of my closest friends, as I had been doing for many years.

Along Lilliam in charitable events

As I've said before, the wedding was a birthday gift to please an aspiration of Lilliam. Because, actually we already had been living together for almost a decade, integrated in many aspects of our lives, although respecting each other's.

One of her activities that I admired most and in which I joined her, without any reservations was the charitable work that Lilliam did for the American Cancer Society.

When she chaired the ACS's Miami chapter, I supported her in everything I could, mostly because I myself already understood the importance of involvement in social welfare benefits, whether it was for low-income children or persons suffering complicated diseases like cancer.

As I have already told, I myself founded in 1998 an ongoing golf tournament for charitable purposes, in Indian Creek, in Miami's northwest, and without knowing that Lilliam was involved with that entity, I donated good money at fund-raising events before meeting her.

Lilliam's commitment to the Cancer Society began after the experience that a nephew-in-law went through, a kid she had seen grow up since he was a four-year-old.

When he was still in his 20s, the young man developed an aggressive form of cancer. He put up a fight along with all his family, winning the battle not once but three times, because the cancer relapsed thrice and until now, he has managed to defeat it. That was the first time that Lilliam had an encounter with cancer, and it was an inspiration for her.

So when her friend Remedios asked her one day to join the efforts of the American Cancer Society, Lilliam didn't think twice.

She organized an endless number of events: lunches, cocktails, and events like Relay for Life, which she created and was held every year in Hialeah, a combination of neighborhood strolls and harvest. She also organized another walk, Making Strikes, to raise funds for the fight against breast cancer.

In those and many other events Lilliam had the opportunity to serve a lot of needy persons. That I can vouch for.

Lilliam's charitable activities did not stop with the American Cancer Society. In 2008 we founded together the Gus Machado Family Foundation Inc., in Hialeah, for the purposed of contributing our grain of sand to society, with emphasis on the neediest.

With the Foundation we organized another series of supporting events for distributing donations. One of the most popular programs was the school fair held at our Gus Machado Ford in Hialeah site, in which more than 400 kids received a backpack filled with school supplies needed for the school year.

During those support activities for the little students a great many bicycles were raffled, and the kids received those with great joy.

Lilliam's sensitivity helped to set in motion other projects that, with my decisive boost, have become my legacy throughout more than six decades.

13

Gus Machado's legacy (2002-2021)

When I earned my first salary in the United States, in the now distant 1952, in Joliet, Illinois, working for Caterpillar, and especially when I established my first business in Hialeah four years later, with a capital of a $2,000 loan from my papa, I never thought that in my trajectory I would leave a lasting historical legacy for the coming years.

Much of what I achieved I naturally owe to my parents, especially my mother Elia Hernández de Machado, from whom I inherited the gift for business, and to my dear brother Ed, who helped me in the crucial moments in which I got my first job in Illinois, thanks to his to his good offices.

My first motivation during those years was to seek the means to support my growing family, and to develop my creative and business capabilities, which I had already discovered in the family farm, thanks to the stimulus from my maternal

Gus and Lilliam Machado, accompanied by Lydia Machado and Víctor Benítez, making a contribution to the Hialeah Gardens High School, an institution founded in 2009.

grandfather, Rafael Calderín.

Then came my distinct interest in the world of advertising, inspired by the good example of Jim Moran, a pioneer who became a central figure by promoting nationwide his own car sales business.

Without foreseeing it I became a public figure and a business reference in the world of Hispanic businesses, with a long series of achievements and recognitions in the industry where I developed.

And beyond my interest for increasing sales, my career and life's driving force; I became aware that as an opinion leader, I could do a lot of good by supporting noble causes to benefit the community.

As I have already explained in previous chapters, I found the inspiration to boost all kinds of projects in promoting local talent, golf tournaments to support charitable causes, all types of fund-raising events, from walks and community celebrations, to gala dinners with Miami's high society.

Encouraged by my wife, Lilliam, I plunged myself in the promotion of the American Cancer Society projects, and with my own organization, the Gus Machado Family Foundation, I materially supported hundreds of low-income families and their children, as a way of giving back a bit of my business success to the people that embraced me in this great nation for most of my life.

And when I was thinking that my time to retire was approaching, new projects arose showing me that I still had much to do.

Social activities of the Gus Machado Family Foundation

By means of the Gus Machado Family Foundation we launched in mid August 2009 the Great Summer Community Fair of Gus Machado Ford, in our Kendall dealership.

We did it there to take advantage of the new business site's recent opening, and meet with the great South Miami community directly.

Along Lilliam we handed out numerous backpacks stuffed with school supplies to the first 100 kids that came to the Fair, a donation that was jointly organized by the Gus Machado Family Foundation and my dear friend Serafín Blanco of El Dolarazo.

It was a great satisfaction for us to see the smiling faces of the kids upon receiving the backpacks that Lilliam was handing out.

The Fair encompassed more than handing out backpacks. Trips to Cancún were raffled, in combination with MK Travel, and the Miami-Dade Health Department, which sent a medical team to vaccinate some 50 kids, thanks to the good offices of Commissioner Joe Martínez.

For their part, the Florida Department of Transportation sent a Mobile Unit to offer license renewals and issue official ID cards for school age children.

It was the first time we did it in Kendall, but we had been arranging this type of events for more than 20 years in Hialeah, for the benefit of our dear community.

Achievements and recognitions with Ford Motor Company

I have always considered that a crucial part of my legacy is the success I have attained, along my partners, family and closest friends, in the difficult and very competitive automobile trade.

I have done everything in the car sales trade: I started

Gus Machado during the 2012 Ford Motor Company Convention in Las Vegas, where he was chosen and awarded as one of the top six worldwide Ford car salesmen.

selling used cars, later I exported these cars first to Cuba, then to Puerto Rico and Argentina.

I was in the business of vehicle rentals and leases in Puerto Rico, a line of business that moves in a very different way in comparison to car sales.

Later I opened a new car sales business, which is the top of the line. The dynamics are absorbent, and you have to dedicate yourself body and soul, with a combination of aggressiveness, friendliness and a lot of imagination, if you want to succeed.

I had several new car agencies; the first one was Buicks and then Fords, both of them in Hialeah. In 2009, I decided to expand my operations with Gus Machado Ford of Kendall, just

Gus Machado is dedicated to countless social causes in greater Miami. His Gus Machado Family Foundation provides critical resources to improve health and education in the community and is closely aligned with the American Cancer Society and important initiatives that raise awareness and fight the disease. The Foundation spearheads a "Relay for Life" event which includes thousands of cancer survivors banding together to raise money for cancer prevention in the Hispanic community. Gus also generously supports R.O.C.K. – Reaching Out to Cancer Kids, which provides summer camps and college scholarships to teenagers stricken with the disease. Mr. Machado also runs annual "Back to School Community Fairs" where hundreds of school-bound children are provided with important essentials including health immunizations and backpacks full of school supplies.

Gus Machado
Gus Machado Ford,
Gus Machado Ford of Kendall
Hialeah, Florida and
Miami, Florida

Biographical sketch of Gus Machado published at the 2012 Ford Convention in Las Vegas, where he received an award as one of the top six dealers worldwide.

after the great real estate bubble that left many belly up.

I was on the verge of bankruptcy, but unlike many others in the trade, I recovered and accomplished a great rebirth that brought me many recognitions and satisfactions.

It was right after natural disasters, particularly hurricane Andrew that the shower of awards began:

For three consecutive years, from 1994 to 1996, we were admitted to the selective One Hundred Club, the exclusive group of the 100 more successful Ford dealerships nationwide, selected from a total of more than 4,300 distributors in the United States.

In 1996, Camacol designated me as Entrepreneur of the Year, an award that put me on the most important spot of the South Florida business community.

That same year, I received in symbolic ceremonies the keys to three cities; Miami, Hialeah and Hialeah Gardens, after having the date of September 28 as Gus Machado Day.

On the following year, 1997, I received two recognitions that were very important for me: Dealer of the Year in Miami-Dade County, and Businessman of the Year granted by the United States Chamber of Commerce of the Southwest, after competing with tens of candidates.

I regarded all these recognitions as well-deserved, because I had dedicated endless hours as a *workaholic* –like my daughter Myra used to label me–, but considering that that was my style I took it in stride.

A new round of recognitions coincided with the advent of the new millenium, when my life was taking a turn on all fronts.

Just on the year when I met Lilliam, in 2001, I received from Ford Motor Company my first Blue Oval Certified.

Two years later, in 2003, I was given the Ford Motor Company's President's Award, for sales performance in my region, a recognition that was only granted to very few dealerships nationwide.

That award marked the highest point of my career as an automobile entrepreneur: it was the top honor that anyone could receive from the Ford home office, granted to 450 dealers chosen out of almost 5,000 Ford and Lincoln Mercury dealerships in the United States and Canada.

In the 2009-2010 period, when I opened the Gus Machado Ford dealership in Kendall, I was given the Partners in Quality Award, granted by Ford to the most loyal and consistent dealers of that great firm.

Ford's Salute to Dealers and 12 "Good Men"

Later came the great recognition awarded by Ford Motor Company to a very selective group of dealers on an international level for their social impact labor, in 2012.

Gus Machado Ford was recognized among only 6 dealerships, including four dealers in the United States (including Gus Machado Ford), one in the Dominican Republic, and the other in the Chinese province of Shanxi.

The text of the recognition dedicated to Gus Machado Ford describes the reasons for being included in that select group:

"Gus Machado is dedicated to endless social causes in Greater Miami. His family's Gus Machado Foundation provides critical resources to improve health and education in the community, and is closely linked to the American Cancer Society and important projects promoting the awareness and fight against that disease."

"The Foundation leads the event Relays for Life, which brings together thousands of cancer survivors for the purpose

Gus Machado was a great activist in the fight for Cuban freedom, along with their great friends Fausto and Remedios Díaz-Oliver and former Representative Ileana Ros-Lehtinen.

of raising funds for the prevention of cancer in the Hispanic community."

Gus Machado, as indicated in the recognition, "has also supported generously the R.O.C.K. (Reaching Out to Cancer Kids), which organizes summer camps and scholarships for teenagers affected by the disease."

"Machado also holds Back to School Community Fairs, in which hundreds of school-aged kids receive essential supplies such as immunization vaccines and backpacks loaded with school supplies."

On the following year, on March 2013, I was included as one of the special guests invited to the prestigious event organized

Gus and Lilliam with former President George W. Bush.

Gus and Representative Ileana Ros-Lehtinen were great allies in the cause of Cuban freedom.

for raising funds for the Ronald McDonald House Charities, which does a great job helping families of sick children.

It was an Annual Lunch honoring 12 South Florida personalities that performed activities of great social impact during the year, particularly for families with sick children.

I was selected as one the dozen outstanding persons selected for the 20thAnnual 12 Good Men Luncheon, held on the Jungle Island Park, who received recognition "for their dedication to the community, civic service and support for local charity works."

That was the end of a good streak of recognitions starting in 1994, which was not at random, but a reward for painstaking work, insistent, occasionally aggressive and disciplined, geared to reach set goals.

Of course, from those times to the present (2021), our businesses continued to be focused on offering a maximum quality service to our customers. That was what, for example, inspired the ambitious projects of expansion and improvement of our stores, which we began in 2017, with a $2 million investment to completely renovate our facilities in the dealerships, a project that without a doubt, judging by the results, was worth it.

During these last decades, my work with Ford was and has been a fundamental part of my work as an entrepreneur. Although it was a crucial part, it did no occupy the totality of my projects and activities. Because my ambitions were not exhausted in the world of car sales, but jumped to other spheres, including political activism for freedom, democratic principle and the fundamental rights consecrated by the Constitution of the United States, particularly on that island where I was born and enslaved by a dictatorship of more of 60 years.

Gus Machado and the Cuban singer Olga Guillot.

My political commitment

When I first came to the United States, a system of free enterprise and broad freedoms reigned in Cuba, although Fulgencio Batista's dictatorship limited the Cubans' political rights.

Everything changed when Castro's revolution took over; throwing the country back to an age of political, economic and social underdevelopment that had already been surpassed by far.

Although I did not live directly under those catastrophic changes brought by Fidel Castro to Cuba, they affected me in diverse ways.

The first impact came when the dictatorship, in power and manifestly socialist, closed the doors on my business of exporting used vehicles to the island.

After that came a more personal impact, when almost all my family still residing in Cuba was forced to seek asylum in Miami, like tens of thousands of Cubans in those years.

The dictatorship's abuses were for me, like for countless Cubans in exile, a thorn driven through the heart. Something, that on the other hand, there wasn't much that could be done to fight it.

During my years as an entrepreneur, when I was committed to succeed in our capitalist system, Cuba's destiny was always on my mind.

There were highly courageous activists, like Jorge Mas Canosa and many other exiled leaders, who devoted their lives to the anti-Castro struggle. They always had my admiration and support. But for my part, I had never thought that I had what it takes to get involved in the political arena.

All that changed in 2003, when by deed and grace of Lilliam and the influence of her friend Remedios Díaz-Oliver, wife of my good friend Fausto Díaz-Oliver, a couple with whom we had cultivated a close friendship for more than a decade.

Gus and Lilliam with former Florida governor and presidential candidate Jeb Bush.

Until that moment, besides the dedication to my business, I had become involved in social activism by way of a wide range of charitable projects, namely the American Cancer Society, where Lilliam had made a career and exerted a great leadership, recognized by all charity circles in South Florida, thanks to Remedios' influence.

But after many conversations with my friends about subjects that concerned Cubans in South Florida, it became clear to me that something significant had to be done to promote freedom in the country where I was born.

A memorable couple

The story of Remedios and Fausto is worth telling. It is similar to mine in many ways, as far as commitment, discipline and dedication to attain success in business; although it also has its own features.

Remedios and Fausto were very young when they came to the United States as exiles, escaping from the Castro dictatorship in mid 1961, weeks after the failed Bay of Pigs invasion.

They left Cuba on the first flight after the conflict, with just the two suitcases they were allowed to bring, and landed in Miami without a penny in their pockets.

They moved to the Northwest part of the city thanks to the help of some friends, and fortunately Fausto started working almost immediately, in a factory where he was paid 75 cents per hour.

Remedios, of course, was one not cut out to stay at home and mind the housework, despite having arrived with a newborn daughter.

She had studied at a prestigious bilingual school in Havana, the Havana Business Academy, a private institution that trained young people for careers in business.

So, when their parents came from the island, three months later, she started job hunting right away. She went to a glass bottle factory near the windows factory where Fausto was already employed, and she was paid $55 for working six days a week.

Gus and the outstanding Cuban-American producer Emilio Estefan.

Curiously, the reason why Remedios chose that job was because they had only one car, a used one that they bought for $59, at the rate of $7 weekly installments.

Although it may sound incredible, after a year on the job, Remedios, who had moved to the administration department, was made vice president of the company.

Certainly, Remedios displayed her talents well. The firm, whose customers were all local, began to spread internationally when Remedios began sale tours all over Central America, including Honduras, El Salvador, Costa Rica, Guatemala and Panamá, selling glass jars for industrial purposes, mostly for beverages. It was a tremendous success and Fausto followed suit.

PAC for freedom

As I mentioned earlier, I met Remedios and Fausto in the '70s, when we ran into each other at a meeting of the *Cámara de Comercio Latina* (Camacol), where Fausto was a vice president for many years, along with Luis Sabines.

Separately, Lilliam and I were friends of Remedios and Fausto for years. But before and after we were married, the relationship between both couples was very tight, and generated more than one interesting project.

One of those was born, without anyone really thinking of it, in mid 2001.

Lilliam and I went to Washington DC for a gala of the

Hispanic Heritage Awards, an organization to which Remedios belonged, and we had been invited as special guests.

The morning before the gala, we went to visit the two Cuban-American members of Congress who represented us: Ileana Ros-Lehtinen and Lincoln Díaz Balart. Both of them received us cheerfully and were pleased by our presence on the capital.

That was during President George W. Bush's government and, naturally, the subject of Cuban freedom was the main topic of our conversations with both members of the House of Representatives.

Both, Ileana and Lincoln expressed their concern for something that impacted us a lot: that the Cuban dictatorship's influence in Congress was growing; that they were spending a lot of money on lobbying; and they feared that laws could be enacted benefitting, one way or another, the communist regime.

"We fear Congress passing laws favorable to the Castro regime, laws that not even President Bush can veto," said Ros-Lehtinen.

When I heard that, which sounded incredible, I felt a tremendous indignation.

"How is it possible for the communists to have so much influence in Washington?" I asked.

That was the first time we talked about the need to do something politically efficient to block that trend.

"The best would be to create a Political Action Committee, a PAC," was the idea that prevailed in those meetings.

Lilliam Machado with her allies Remedios Díaz-Oliver and Florida Attorney General Katherine Fernández-Rundle.

Until that moment I had never dabbled directly in politics, but I felt that perhaps it was time to do so.

We ended the meeting with the representatives, and got ready for the Hispanic Heritage awards gala that evening.

The event included an artistic show at the Kennedy Center, and it presented artists of the caliber Celia Cruz and Gloria Estefan; and a gala dinner at the Watergate Hotel.

At dinner time we coincided with a young man of Cuban extraction who was speaking passionately about freedom in Cuba.

Everything he was saying about what was happening on the island at present, and what had to be done, coincided with what we had been discussing earlier that day with the representatives.

The young man was Mauricio Claver-Carone, at the moment a talented lawyer working at the Treasury Department as advisor on regulatory subjects related to banking and finances.

"Mauricio is saying exactly what we are thinking," commented Remedios.

"I agree," was my reply, and the enthusiasm for what Mauricio had been saying was such that the conversation lasted until 3 a.m.

After that evening, we were all convinced that we had a moral obligation to help our country, and give soul, life and heart so that our native country could one day be free.

Almost immediately we decided to ask Mauricio to head the project of creating a PAC. But Claver-Carone declined arguing that he was working on something "very important" at the Treasury Department, and did not want to abandon that position.

However, he asked us to give him "a little time" to make a decision.

A few months later, in November 2001, on the occasion of my birthday celebrations at a Miami theatre, with a show that included the presentation of my good friend the impersonator Julio Sabala, we ran again into Mauricio Claver-Carone.

Again the subject of the PAC came up, and Mauricio said he was ready to accept if he was given a bit more time to wrap up

Fausto and Remedios Díaz-Oliver, great friends of Gus and Lillian Machado.

ongoing tasks.

The moment finally arrived a year and a half later. In June 2003, we registered the US-Cuba Democracy Political Action Committee, headed by Mauricio and in which I had a role as treasurer.

A patriotic feeling

When we registered the For Cuba's Freedom PAC we immediately started contacting our friends and acquaintances to begin the hard work of fund raising.

Until that moment the most active organization in the United States for promoting the Cuban cause was the Cuban-

American National Foundation, founded by Jorge Mas Canosa in 1981, but by 2003 anti- Castro activism was not at its best.

What we endeavored was to organize a team to visit Congress on a daily basis, speak to its leaders every day, to show them the truth about what was going on in Cuba.

We had to counter the enemies of the free Cuba cause, who were moving at ease on the power corridors of Washington and especially in Congress, because there were congressmen, Democrats as well as Republicans, who refused to support the cause of freedom on the island.

That's why Mauricio was the key person, because he knew the nooks and crannies of power in Washington, and was very active and well respected, and because over the years he had built excellent relations with many congressmen.

So I began my fund-raising job with a lot of enthusiasm and effort, driven by the love I still felt for my mother country.

Along with Remedios, Lilliam and Fausto, we began to organize fund- raising events. We explained to everyone that 100 percent of their donations went directly to assist the congressmen who were friendly to our common cause, instead of covering superfluous expenses.

"No one is going to get any money out of this; neither will the money go to defray travel expenses nor meals. Everything is going to helping the cause," I explained to the friends and acquaintances that approached us in the fund-raising events.

One time we organized an event in Orlando, where the people

participated very generously, and we collected a significant amount of money. I could not attend, but was able to count on the help of Mauricio Claver's mother and grandmother, who lived there. It was an incredibly patriotic feeling because the donations came from doctors, entrepreneurs, common people who lived in Orlando and were very intent about the Cuban cause.

Another time we organized an event in Puerto Rico, thanks to the help of a very active Cuban, Eduardo Pérez Bengoechea. In that event nearly $65,000 was raised.

Another event I recall was held in Atlanta, where Congressman Mario Díaz-Balart, a great friend of the cause, who had been elected as a representative the year before, was present.

The PAC turned the Miami-Dade County Auditorium into a very popular annual fund-raising show, with the participation of Cuban great stars, the likes of Albita, Malena Burke and Paquito D'Rivera, who did not charged us a penny for their performances.

In a short time, we started gaining the support of congressmen from both parties, who began to understand the true nature of Cuba's communist dictatorship, and were convinced that it was necessary to act.

One of the most memorable events was the one we organized at the Coral Gables Biltmore Hotel. We brought as one of the main speakers a former Cuban political prisoner, Eusebio Peñalver, who exposed bluntly the situation that Afro-Cubans were facing in Fidel Castro's Cuba.

One of the congressmen invited to that event was Representative George K. Butterfield (D-NC), who was deeply impressed by the testimony of the mulatto Eusebio, who had spent 20 years in Castro's prisons.

In his exposé, Peñalver explained how Blacks were mistreated Cuba, and had no opportunities for improvement; he gave many examples of discrimination, and demonstrated convincingly that everything Castro said about the Blacks on the island was false.

"How come there aren't more Black Cubans exiled in the United States?" asked the congressman, very intrigued by the subject.

"Because, unfortunately, they have no way of leaving, they don't have relatives here to sponsor them or send them any money, and they cannot afford to pay for the travel expenses," answered the former political prisoner.

After that exchange, Butterfield, like many other politicians and congressmen, became an unconditional ally of the cause of Cuban freedom.

The work of promoting this cause and winning key and diverse allies, from so many different places, against the Castro dictatorship, was a most satisfactory endeavor.

Of course, we could always count on the unconditional support of our Florida representatives, like Ileana Ros-Lehtinen, the brothers Lincoln and Mario Díaz-Balart, Marco Rubio and the rest of the congressmen who came later and are still active.

But we also received the crucial support of congressmen from across the political spectrum.

That was the case of Congresswoman Debbie Wasserman Schultz, ex- president of the Democratic Party, who had been a great friend of the PAC, the free Cuba cause and of other countries also suffering the evils of communism, like Venezuela and Nicaragua.

Another remarkable case is the Democrat Congressman Albio Sires, born in Bejucal (like actor Andy García), in the Mayabeque province, who left Cuba at the age of 11, a decent and upright man who has kept his struggle against communism in Cuba, and who has given us a great support for the PAC throughout the years.

A tireless anti-Castro fighter has been Senator Bob Menéndez (D-NY), a friend of the PAC practically since its inception.

We cannot forget, among many others, Congressman Alex Mooney, from West Virginia, born in United States, with a Cuban mother who escaped from Fidel Castro's dictatorship, and planted on her children the ideals of struggle against communist dictatorships.

When I'm asked what has been the great accomplishment of the Freedom for Cuba PAC for the past two decades, I summarize it this way:

"The most important thing the PAC has achieved is that the

sanctions against Castro's Cuba have not been lifted."

As everybody knows, the so-called "blockade" reviled by the Havana dictatorship as the main reason for the great evils punishing Cubans, is a great lie, because the United States does not prevent Cuba from trading with anyone they want, including American companies.

The detail is that the dictatorship, thanks to those sanctions, does not have access to international credit. One of the PAC's great battles was to make sure that no credit be extended to Castro regime which had confiscated the properties of all the American companies which were doing business in Cuba in the decade of the '60s, and never compensated them.

There were never enough votes to eliminate those sanctions. Not even Barack Obama, who wanted to lift the sanctions during his presidency, was able to garner the necessary votes in Congress to suspend the sanctions, thanks in part to the meticulous work of our PAC, and of people like Mauricio Claver, Remedios Díaz-Oliver and our dear supporters in Congress.

I consider the PAC's legacy as one of the more outstanding achievements of my trajectory of 70 years in the United States.

The Gus Machado Way

One of the recognitions I have proudly kept is the resolution approved on December 2011 by the City of Hialeah, to designate one of the city streets as Gus Machado Way.

Gus Machado, his wife Lilliam and his daughter Lydia Machado at the dedication of the Gus Machado Way, approved to honor him by the City of Hialeah, in June 2012.

According to Resolution 11-133, the Way was designated as a portion of West 13th Lane between West 44th Place and West 47th Place, and West 47th Place from West 13th Lane and West 12th Avenue.

For me the most satisfactory part were the reasons backing the resolution:

"Gus Machado has been an entrepreneur, philanthropist and community leader in the City of Hialeah since 1982."

"In 2003, Gus Machado founded the US-Cuba Democracy PAC, a political group promoting an unconditional transition towards democracy, the recognition of basic human and civil rights and free market in Cuba." And, finally,

"In 2008, Machado created the Gus Machado Family Foundation, a non-profit organization dedicated to philanthropy, volunteer work and the granting of scholarships and funds for important causes."

The resolution was ratified a month after, on January 24, 2012, by the Board of Commissioners of Miami-Dade County, a recognition for which I shall always be grateful.

However, another kind of legacy has always grabbed my lifelong interest in an area which I also consider vital in the long run: the education of the new generations.

14

Finishing touch: The Gus Machado Business School

Throughout my years in the world of philanthropy, I supported all kinds of social welfare projects regardless of who were the recipients. I donated my efforts and my money to organize activities such as prestigious golf competitions, gala dinners, walks and market festivals.

I promoted causes in which I believed, and enthused many of my wealthy friends and neighbors to give their part for good social causes.

I helped collecting money for the American Cancer Society projects, first in an institutional manner by sponsoring golf tournaments, and afterwards thanks to enthusiasm of my wife Lilliam, who for years chaired the organization's South Florida chapter.

I organized events to help and promote talented young artists, in competitions that were broadcast on TV.

It was something about which I felt very comfortable, especially because music and dance have played an important role throughout my life.

I participated actively in political causes for Cuba's freedom, because despite having lived the greater part of my life in this great country, we Cubans never stop feeling a strong link with the land where we were born.

However, one of the projects that has motivated me the most in my career has been helping young people who are striving to get ahead in life.

I started with my own kids, to whom I tried to give the best possible opportunities so that they could lead a productive life.

Later we began with programs to donate school supplies, and we did that for years to benefit the young students of Hialeah.

I have always been a firm believer in giving back to society a part of what one has received in this great country. I always felt the need to help others succeed, in the same way that many have helped me achieve success as an entrepreneur.

So the new project that I undertook since 2015 came to me unexpectedly, but it was no surprise. It was as if the occasion opened the doors for me, and I went in full blast towards the future it offered me.

Monsignor Casale's good luck

The new educational project's proposal came at random

Gus Machado during a visit to the site of the future Business School, named after him at St. Thomas University, in 2020.

–or by God's mysterious ways– from the hands of my dear and respected friend Monsignor Franklyn Casale, Honorary President of St. Thomas University (STU).

I knew Father Casale from before, in the many charitable events both of us attended.

Monsignor Casale was highly committed, in his characteristic style since he assumed STU's presidency in 1994, to further elevate the level of his dear house of studies, managed by the Miami Archdiocese, with a new business school.

I was particularly interested in the history and the projects of that Catholic university because it had a strong connection with Cuba.

STU was born originally in Havana as the *Universidad Católica de Santo Tomás de Villanueva*, under the administration of the Augustine Order. When the dictatorship took over, Fidel Castro ordered the confiscation of its buildings and grounds, and expelled from the island the entire religious and academic faculty.

The Augustinians came to Miami and refounded the university under the name of Biscayne College. In 1984, the school was renamed St. Thomas University, and four years later, in 1988, the Miami Archdiocese, led by Archbishop Edward Anthony McCarthy, offered its sponsorship.

Monsignor Casale became the ninth president of STU in April 1994. I met him years later and identified myself very much with his style, because like me, he considered himself a troubleshooter for other people.

He came from a New Jersey family used to overcoming difficulties, similar to the family environment in which I grew up, although in completely different situations.

His family had to endure the dreadful times of the Depression years, an experience which marked young Franklyn's life, and eventually led him to his vocation.

I did not have a religious formation, but we coincided on a very important subject: the best way to help people is by offering them opportunities for the highest education level.

I cooperated a lot with Father Casale's tasks. We were always attentive to his calls, in order to support him in whatever was

Gus and Lilliam Machado next to Monsignor Franklyn Casale, President Emeritus of St. Thomas University, during the blessing ceremony of the Gus Machado Business School at that university, in 2020.

within our reach.

One day he called us with a proposal. He wanted to include me on STU's Board of Trustees.

With the utmost respect, I replied:

"Look, Monsignor, you can count on me to continue contributing my donations for the growth of the university. But I cannot sit on the board, because I have to mind car sales 24/7," I explained.

Monsignor smiled and said no more.

But shortly after, he called us again to invite the Machado family to a luncheon at the university. I went with Lilliam, my partner Víctor Benítez, my daughter Lydia, and my secretary Ana Arisso.

Present at that lunch, besides Monsignor Casale were other members of the university's Board of Directors.

After enjoying a lunch of salmon, rice and a pleasant chat, Monsignor Casale took me aside a said that he wanted a few minutes with Lilliam and I.

Lilliam turned and said:

"Víctor, I want you to come with us."

We went to Casale's Spartan office, where his assistant was present, and Monsignor began to explain the motive for the meeting:

"We have been considering all the elements and have decided that the university should have a business school," he said.

"We're planning to build a building complex to house the school, and state of the art technology to educate young entrepreneurs with an ethical focus," he continued.

"We are planning to build a special classroom with computers, a laboratory for commercial transactions with high technology equipment to be used by all the students."

We were listening attentively.

"I would like to know if Gus Machado and his family are willing to support us donating the money to help build that technological business center which, of course, would bear his name," he added.

The three of us stared at each other. We knew that Monsignor

The St. Thomas University Business School will preserve for future generations the managerial legacy of Gus Machado.

Casale wanted to present us a proposal for support of the university's activities, an idea that we were more than willing to back.

But at the moment I didn't comprehend fully what Father Casale had meant. So I asked:

"You mean a classroom?"

"Yes, naming a classroom after you," replied the priest. "Monsignor... and just how much would that be?"

Casale began to discuss the this and that about the issue,

and after many explanations, gave us a figure:

"The estimated cost is half a million dollars."

"That's what you need for a classroom?" I asked anew. "That's it, Don Gus," replied the priest.

Then, I stood up from the chair, and without thinking much about it, threw him another question:

"And how much would the whole school cost?"

Monsignor Casale moved back on his executive chair, somewhat disconcerted, and replied to my question with another question:

"You mean the whole school?" he said.

"Yes," I replied. "Because, after all, what are you going to do with just one classroom?"

Without a doubt, my question had jolted Father Casale, who was left practically speechless.

"It's not a classroom. You need to build the whole school," I continued.

Monsignor was still dazed. After a few seconds, he took a deep breath and managed to say:

"Mr. Machado, give me some time to answer."

When we left, I got in the car with my wife. Once alone, Lilliam said: "Gus, do you realize what you said to Monsignor?"

"Yes, chica," I replied. "Because, what's Monsignor going to do with a single classroom? He needs the whole school!"

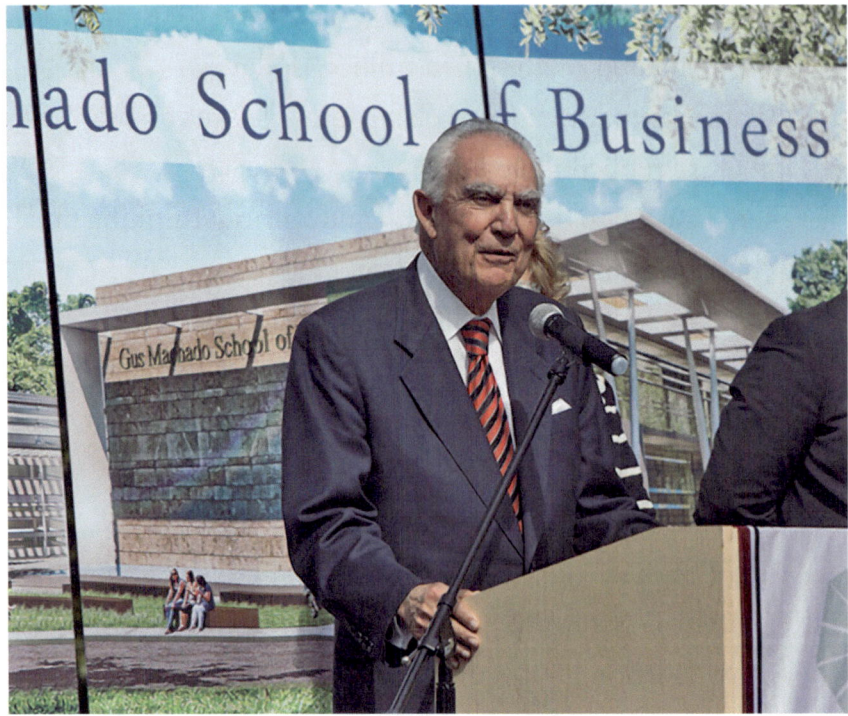

The Gus Machado Business School opened in 2020 for the benefit of thousands of South Florida students who would like to follow the example of the great Hialeah businessman.

Education at the highest level

What perhaps could have been a contribution of $500,000 for the construction of a hall for business and technology studies, according to Monsignor Casale's initial proposal, turned out to be an enormous project, for which I felt especially honored to donate $5 million.

Without wanting to brag, it was the biggest donation

received by STU in its entire history, up to that moment, and I believe the record still stands as of today.

Almost immediately, a few weeks after the meeting with the priest, the project was anounced:

"Thanks to his generous donation, the new Gus Machado Business School of St. Thomas University shall give our business students the potential to assume business challenges with free market based solutions, and rise as ethical leaders in the global market," stated Monsignor Casale during an act in which the project was announced, early in July 2015.

Later he added something that sounded like a compliment:

"Gus Machado is a highly respected man in our community. His generosity will make it possible for our institution to offer a first class education in business, based on values."

On my part, I made very clear the importance of this project for me.

"Supporting the future business leaders is highly significant for me. To enable that at St. Thomas University, a university that enjoys a reputation of providing an excellent educational experience, and of developing the new generations of ethical business leaders, is an opportunity of which I am very pleased to participate."

In a statement to The Miami Herald, I also said reflexively:

"This is going to help young people. You only live once and no one takes anything with him when the time comes. When that time comes, you leave and that's it."

Víctor Benítez, General Manager of Gus Machado Ford, David A. Armstrong, President of St. Thomas University, Lilliam and Gus Machado, and Father Rafael Capó, during the blessing of the Gus Machado Business School, in 2020.

Monsignor Casale got to work without wasting any time. The complex's design was commissioned to Bermello Ajamil & Partners, of Miami. He got more donors for the ambitious structure, including a $1.6 million from John Dooner, STU's chairman of the board, and $1 million from the entrepreneur and *alumnus* Jorge Rico.

Casale not only secured the grounds for building the complex, a total of 144 acres in Miami Gardens, but he also organized the complicated academic aspects of the new school, which would be offering several programs for college and graduate students at a higher level.

On January 24, 2018, two and a half years after that lunch at STU, the ground-breaking ceremony took place to formally kick-off the construction of the complex that would house the business school named after me.

The ceremony was a very significant act. University authorities and important regional leaders were there, among them my friends the Congressman Mario Díaz-Balart and the former coach of the Miami Dolphins, Don Shula.

Lilliam and I accompanied Monsignor Casale and other university authorities in a beautiful symbolic act, consisting of moving a bit of soil with a shovel to represent the beginning of the construction work.

At the time, the new school plans were fairly well drawn and advanced.

The Business School would be the last great project driven by Monsignor Casale in his 24-year trajectory as president of STU.

When the first works started to set the foundations of the complex, Monsignor Franklyn Casale had already initiated his retirement, after reaching the age of 75.

A long term job

The torch of the Gus Machado Business School, which Monsignor Casale had lit and promoted since 2014, was relayed on 2018 to another highly active personality for whom I feel

A view of the St. Thomas University Gus Machado Business School, a project to which Gus and Lilliam Machado donated $5 millions.

great respect: David Armstrong.

David was chosen as Monsignor Casale's successor and he got to work on it on February 2018, with the same enthusiasm as his predecessor. Lilliam and I developed a great relationship with him from the very beginning of his tenure.

As foreseen, the works concluded by mid 2020, two and a half years after the groundbreaking ceremony. Not even the effects of the Covid-19 pandemic, which caused unexpected delays, were able to stop the grand project's culmination.

The structure of the school was designed with a great futuristic, and practical, style, taking in consideration esthetics, comfort, illumination and amplitude aspects.

The final cost of the complex, which stretches to a total area of more than 46,000 square feet, with a capacity to house 1,600 students, was $21.5 million. The academic building has 20 classrooms, an auditorium, a studio for conferences and video transmissions, and an area dedicated to incubate the students' business projects (the classroom which Monsignor Casale had originally offered me for financing).

A second building was also constructed, to house the faculty offices and a large conference room for the board of directors.

Also included was a sky bridge connecting both buildings, with an innovative design style.

When I learned the academic details, I was totally surprised by the advances made for the formation of young entrepreneurs.

The new business school named after me offers so many tools that we never dreamed of having in my times, when the entrepreneur was made on the job with the day-to-day practice.

Of course, today's reality is far more complex for the entrepreneurs, who have to know a bit of everything to face the challenges of doing business in a globalized world.

It was the world I had to face, in which I was forced to learn on the job all about accounting, management, promotion strategies to increase sales, bureaucratic procedures to obtain building or exportation permits; taxes and commissions for salesmen, mortgage loans and even the laws in order to avoid possible lawsuits.

Fortunately, the young entrepreneurs-to-be can count on

Gus Machado delivers a few words of gratitude along with his wife Lilliam during the Boys & Girls Club of Broward Awards Gala, in 2022.

many more and better tools from the STU business school.

In general, the school offers 39 programs for college students and graduate and doctoral students in 11 areas of specialization, including Cybersecurity, Accounting, Financing, Marketing and Sports Administration, for those who want to make a business life in the sports sector.

One of the school's approaches that I am in complete agreement with is to provide the future entrepreneur not only with knowledge that is theoretical but practical as well, by way of internships that create an interactive environment which can prepare the student for the real world.

Another approach is the idea of offering classes to smaller student groups (no more than 15 students per class), so that they can receive an education updated to the particular needs of each one of them. The result will be, without any doubt, a student with better opportunities for preparing for the highest possible academic level.

Finally, and this I believe is already part of the essence of the St. Thomas University Business School that carries my name, to include also an education in leadership and business ethics. These are two essential aspects for the success in business activities, like it was for my own career as a businessman for more than 60 years.

My legacy and my American Dream

The official inauguration official of the Gus Machado Business School, October 16, 2020, was an extraordinary event.

The ceremonial mass was celebrated by the Archbishop of the Miami Archdiocese, Thomas Wensky, with the presence of the University of St. Thomas President, David Armstrong, and our dear Monsignor Franklyn Casale, now designated President *Emeritus* of the house of studies.

I was accompanied to the event by my wife Lilliam and my partner Víctor Benítez, who was also involved in the project from the beginning.

During the dedication mass, Monsignor Wensky spoke

Gus and Lilliam Machado at the launching of the campaign for the construction of the St. Thomas University Gus Machado Business School, July 2015.

about the need for the entrepreneur to go beyond searching for efficiency in business, and making it an activity for seeking personal integrity and holiness.

"To be an entrepreneur should be a vocation, a way of responding to the baptismal calling for holiness, to be with the world instead of being the world," said the Miami archbishop.

David Armstrong, President of STU, addressed the organizational aspect of the business school.

"The Gus Machado complex has two transformative strategies. First comes forming a corporate alliance to create a new type of business school in Florida, focused on business and ethics; and secondly, to benefit the students as well as all the South Florida community."

My wife Lilliam expressed with grand and simple words my feelings at that moment:

"This is a dream come true for my husband. The entire family is very proud that he will make a difference in the life of so many people," she said.

During the ceremony I couldn't avoid remembering my own past as a young entrepreneur, who needed all the help he could get to reach success in a competitive environment.

Like I said during the inauguration ceremony:

"I have always enjoyed helping the young population, helping them to rise and improve themselves."

The Business School is, at the journey's end, the finishing touch for my legacy of 60 years living and striving in this land of liberty, prosperity and hope, making a reality of the legendary American Dream of Gus Machado.

15

Epilogue: Memories of my Father

*By Myra Dewhurst **

The memories of my childhood, of growing up as Gus Machado's first born are powerful and, although seeming so distant, so many decades later, those memories have always been a part of my daily life.

Dad was a young father with unlimited energy and enthusiasm, but he still had much to learn while juggling to make ends meet by the end of the month, while building a business and supporting a family.

Dad worked many hours, six days a week (Monday through Saturday). Often he was not at home during the week, since he got up and left early and not returned home until late at night. But he always made an effort to reserve Sundays for family time. Those special Sundays were very important for the unity of our family.

That invaluable family time on Sundays often included

Gus Machado surrounded by his sons and daughters Roberto, Myra, Lydia and Rudolph Machado, in the summer of 2008.

visiting our grandparents, my mother's parents, Lola and Pepe. We used to visit their Miami Beach apartment, three blocks from South Beach, and we could walk to and from the beach.

We enjoyed swimming and splashing into the water from his shoulders; the beach was a terrific playground for us kids.

Moreover, Sundays were special because mom made a great breakfast that we enjoyed together on Sunday mornings.

Our play time on the beach ended with a delicious meal prepared by mom Olga and our grandmother Lola. Our favorites were the grilled shrimp and the Spanish omelettes.

Another Sunday gift was watching TV together on Sunday evenings. We loved The Wonderful World of Color (with

Walt Disney), followed by dad's beloved westerns (that he still watches). We loved Bonanza, followed by The High Chaparral.

It was also one of the rare occasions in which we were sometimes treated to ice cream (Neapolitans).

We passed our vacations with family and friends, visiting and sharing good food, good music, memories, traditions and good times.

Love for laughter, music, dance and singing

My father has always been young at heart and enjoyed making others laugh, joking and being playful. He was very young (just 18) when he became a father. I was the first born, on February 21, 1953; followed by Rudy, on April 19, 1954; Lydia on May 21, 1955 and Robert, who arrived on July 30, 1956.

His youth's energy, his hopes and dreams, along with a very positive perspective for the future, as well as the help from family members and friends, made possible, in the middle of very challenging circumstances, with a little money and support, the life of a young family in a new land.

Dad always felt a great love for music, dancing and singing. He loved parties, celebrations, music, dance, conversations and connections. He always liked it when the others had as much fun as he did.

I remember that on one occasion, he brought home some percussion instruments and we had a lot of fun trying to play

Lilliam with Gus Machado and daughters Lydia, Myra and her husband Henry Dewhurst, at the Ford Motor Company's 2012 Award presented to Gus in Las Vegas.

them along with the music from the record player.

My father always made everything possible to support local musicians, hiring them to promote his business, as well as for parties; he also used to tip street performers, something I always admired.

Ready to solve problems

Dad is a troubleshooter and has always been keen on helping his family, friends and neighbors to get out of challenging situations.

He's a good listener. He believes in taking responsibility

for his mistakes, showing a genuine effort to remedy them.

He's convinced that everyone deserves an opportunity to learn from their mistakes and improve their lives.

Although dad worked many hours, his family could always count on him to help them solve challenging situations.

As it often happens, in the process of growing up, life gets complicated by the many challenges of growing up, combined with the inexperience of youth. And dad always made time to help us solve our problems.

Unlimited generosity

Gus was and still is a risk-taker who succeeded most of the times. His confidence and hard work served him well in his quest for the American Dream.

My father's positive attitude and energy has been a powerful teacher giving us hope in so many possibilities. Even though failures can be unavoidable, the way in which we choose to deal with failure can teach us to reevaluate ourselves and can make us better people in the long run.

My father has a genuine love for people and wants to know everybody's story. He connects with a lot of people because he is capable of finding and nourishing things that they share in common, and made many connections throughout his life.

Dad's ability to tell a good story or making a funny joke has endeared him to many people.

Dad loves happy endings and he strives to do what it takes to make that happen in everyone's life.

Dad's generosity towards those in need is evident in his many contributions to several community organizations, as well as to countless people who have been going through difficult times.

I am very proud of his work to fight cancer (which killed his brother); and for his contribution to the construction of the St. Thomas University Business School.

He has great memories and love for his Cuban childhood, as well as for the powerful Cuban culture. My father also feels

Gus and Lilliam Machado next to Lydia, granddaughter Samantha Dewhurst, Myra and her husband Hank, during the dedication of the Gus Machado Way by the City of Hialeah, in June 2012.

Gus and Lilliam Machado during a baseball game sponsored by Gus Machado Ford at the Marlins Stadium in 2014, accompanied by Fausto and Remedios Díaz-Olivier, Lydia Machado, Víctor Benítez and his wife Idania.

great sadness for the current political situation in Cuba and has done a lot of work to promote the freedom of expression and access to information on the island.

But he has prided himself on, and loved his decision to embrace his American identity.

For this and everything else, I love my father.

(*) Myra Dewhurst is Gus Machado's oldest daughter. This text was originally written in 2021.

Made in the USA
Columbia, SC
10 July 2024